The Age of Augustus

The Age of Augustus

Werner Eck

Translated by Deborah Lucas Schneider
New material by Sarolta A. Takács

Blackwell
Publishing

© 1998 by Verlag C. H. Beck oHG, München
Additional material for this edition copyright © 2003 Sarolta A. Takács
Translation copyright © 2003 Deborah Lucas Schneider

BLACKWELL PUBLISHING
350 Main Street, Malden, MA 02148-5020, USA
9600 Garsington Road, Oxford OX4 2DQ, UK
550 Swanston Street, Carlton, Victoria 3053, Australia

First published in German under the title *Augustus und seine Zeit* 1998
First published in English 2003 by Blackwell Publishing Ltd

3   2005

Library of Congress Cataloging-in-Publication Data
Eck, Werner.
[Augustus und seine Zeit. English]
The age of Augustus / Werner Eck; translated by Deborah Lucas
Schneider; new material by Sarolta A. Takács.
p. cm.
Includes bibliographical references and index.
ISBN 0-631-22957-4 (hbk) – ISBN 0-631-22958-2 (pbk)
1. Augustus, Emperor of Rome, 63 BC–14 AD. 2. Rome – History –
Augustus, 30 BC–14 AD. 3. Emperors – Rome – Biography.
I. Schneider, Deborah Lucas. II. Takács, Sarolta A. III. Title.
DG279 .E2513 2003
937.07092 – dc21
2002005373

ISBN-13: 978-0-631-22957-5 (hbk) – ISBN-13: 978-0-631-22958-2 (pbk)

A catalogue record for this title is available from the British Library.

Set in 11.5 on 13.5 pt Bembo
by SNP Best-set Typesetter Ltd, Hong Kong
Printed and bound in the United Kingdom
by TJ International, Padstow, Cornwall

The publisher's policy is to use permanent paper from mills that operate a
sustainable forestry policy, and which has been manufactured from pulp
processed using acid-free and elementary chlorine-free practices. Furthermore,
the publisher ensures that the text paper and cover board used have met
acceptable environmental accreditation standards.

For further information on Blackwell Publishing, visit our website:
www.blackwellpublishing.com

Contents

Contents

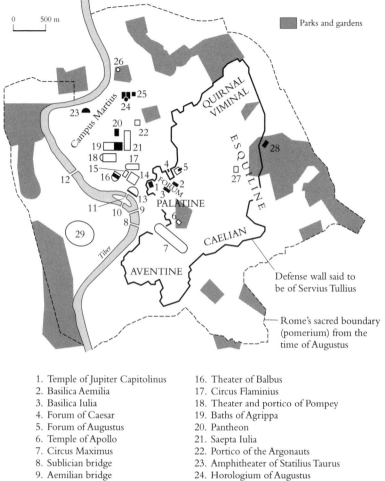

Parks and gardens

0   500 m

26

QUIRNAL
VIMINAL

25
24

23
Campus Martius

20   22
19   21
18   17
15   4 5
16 14 2
12   1 FORUM
        3
        PALATINE
13
11 10 9
    8

29

ESQUILINE
28

27

Tiber

7   CAELIAN

AVENTINE

Defense wall said to
be of Servius Tullius

Rome's sacred boundary
(pomerium) from the
time of Augustus

1. Temple of Jupiter Capitolinus
2. Basilica Aemilia
3. Basilica Iulia
4. Forum of Caesar
5. Forum of Augustus
6. Temple of Apollo
7. Circus Maximus
8. Sublician bridge
9. Aemilian bridge
10. Cestian bridge
11. Fabrician bridge
12. Bridge of Agrippa
13. Theater of Marcellus
14. Portico of Octavia
15. Portico of Philip

16. Theater of Balbus
17. Circus Flaminius
18. Theater and portico of Pompey
19. Baths of Agrippa
20. Pantheon
21. Saepta Iulia
22. Portico of the Argonauts
23. Amphitheater of Statilius Taurus
24. Horologium of Augustus
25. Altar of Peace
26. Mausoleum of Augustus
27. Portico of Livia
28. Market of Livia
29. Naumachia of Augustus

Map 1 Rome in the Augustan period (from J.-P. Martin, *La Rome
ancienne*, PUF, 1973)

North Sea

BRITANNIA

GERMANIA

Atlantic Ocean

Batavi
Kalkriese
Haltern
Cherusci
Oberaden

Ubii
Sugambri
Mogontiacum Taunus
Marktbreit

Seine
Loire
Rhine
Moselle
Neckar
Main
Elbe
Marcomanni

GALLIA
COMATA
Danube

Carnuntum
RAETIA NORICUM

GALLIA
TRANSPADANA
VENETIA
ET HISTRIA PANNONIA
Drau

GALLIA
NARBONENSIS
LIGURIA 2
3
Save
ILLYRICUM

Astures Cantabri

HISPANIA
Duero
TARRACONENSIS

LUSITANIA

BAETICA

Emerita
Tajo

Gades

Massilia
Rubicon

ETRURIA
Adriatic

4
UMBRIA

Roma
5
SAMNIUM
6
CAMPANIA
7
8
10
9

12
13

Tarraco

CORSICA

SARDINIA

SICILIA

Mediterranean Sea

AFRICA PROCONSULARIS

Gaetuli

1 Mantua
2 Mutina
3 Bononia
4 Perusia
5 Velitrae
6 Circei
7 Beneventum
8 Nola
9 Misenum
10 Tarentum
11 Brundisium
12 Naulochus
13 Mylae

0   500 km

Garamantes

Map 2   The Roman Empire

MOESIA

THRACE

Philippi

MACEDONIA

Apollonia

Corcyra

Actium

Iicopolis

ACHAIA

Atheps

Byzantium

Samus

Miletus

Kyme

ASIA

GALATIA

PAPHLAGONIA

PONTUS

Black Sea

Ancyra

Antiochia

Apollonia

Taurus

PAMPHYLIA

Lycia

Limyra

CILICIA

RHODOS

CYPRUS

CRETA

Mediterranean Sea

IUDAEA

Alexandria

AEGYPTUS

Nile

Jordan

SYRIA

Carrhae

Parthians

Euphrates

Tigris

ARMENIA

?Artagira

Albani

Caucasus

IBERIA

Danube

Tisza

1
Augustus' Career in Overview: The Res Gestae

Late in the year AD 14 a large parcel from Rome arrived in Ancyra (present-day Ankara), capital of the Roman province of Galatia-Pamphylia in the heart of Anatolia. It was addressed to the provincial governor and had been sent by the consuls – still the highest-ranking officials of the Roman state, at least in name. They informed the governor that after the princeps Augustus had died and been deified, his last will and testament had been read aloud in the Senate. The will included the princeps' own account of his accomplishments and the gifts he had made to the Roman people from his own funds – an account now known as the *Res Gestae Divi Augusti* ("The Accomplishment of the Divine Augustus"). The consuls reported that, as Augustus had directed, the text of the *Res Gestae* had been engraved on two bronze pillars and placed in front of his mausoleum. This seemed insufficient, however, since the tribute would be limited to Rome. Therefore the Senate had decreed that its contents should also be made known to residents of the provinces, and the recipient would find a copy enclosed.

How the governor carried out the Senate's decree in the short term is not known. Perhaps he summoned the residents of the capital to the theater or the marketplace to hear a reading of the text translated into Greek. What we do know, however, is that he did not stop there. The governor made sure that the words of the late ruler were widely circulated in his province and ultimately carved in stone. In the town of Ancyra itself, craftsmen inscribed the text of the *Res Gestae* in both Latin and Greek on the walls of a temple to Roma and Augustus. Scholars refer to it as the *Monumentum Ancyranum*, and the historian Theodor Mommsen called it the "queen of inscriptions."

The text of the *Res Gestae* provides a self-portrait of the first princeps of Rome as he wished himself and his achievements to be remembered. At the age of nineteen, he wrote, he had entered Roman politics abruptly, acting "on his own initiative" and "at his own expense." As he finished revising the text of the *Res Gestae*, in the seventy-sixth year of his life, he was still the dominant figure on the political scene. The process begun on his own initiative soon received the blessing of the Senate – even though that blessing was coerced rather than voluntary. Even in old age Augustus recalled all the many offices and functions that the Senate and the people had entrusted to him, and provided a detailed list of them. No one before him had attained a comparable position in the Roman state; no one else had achieved so many triumphs or received so many honors.

Having extended the sovereign territory of the Roman people in every direction, Augustus also asserted Roman dominance over peoples whose territories he did not incorporate from astute tactical considerations. Under his leadership the empire attained previously unknown levels of might, stability, and prestige both internally and externally, so that delegations arrived to pay homage from peoples as far away as the Albanians and Iberians in the Caucasus Mountains, and from monarchs in India. The Senate and people of Rome had recognized his unparalleled achievements by devising entirely new honors for him. The Senate granted him the name

Augustus and adorned the entrance to his house with laurel trees and the civic crown. It also placed on display in the Curia Iulia, the chamber where it met, a golden shield engraved with Augustus' virtues: *virtus* (valor), *clementia* (clemency), *iustitia* (justice), and *pietas* (piety; observance of one's duty toward both gods and fellow men). His possession of these qualities was declared the foundation for his exalted rank. Bestowal of the title "father of the country" (*pater patriae*) was the logical consequence and final proof of his supreme position as *princeps*, the first man in the state.

How the inhabitants of Galatia reacted to this self-assessment of their late ruler, we do not know. Much of it was already familiar; they had been told again and again about the superhuman feats Augustus had performed. City officials everywhere in the province had passed resolutions honoring their distant lord and erected statues of him. They had built altars before which residents of the province assembled every year to swear an oath of loyalty to him and his children, promising to protect him even at the cost of their own lives. For nearly 40 years Augustus had represented to the people of Galatia the far-off ruler who demanded taxes but also guaranteed the peace: a figure on a plane above ordinary mortals.

After his death Romans also discussed the extraordinary position he had occupied: his unparalleled thirteen elections to the consulate, his 21 acclamations as *imperator* (victorious commander) and the new honors invented especially for him. About a hundred years later, however, the historian Tacitus dismissed them as superficial, because all these titles, honors, and the long list of tributes and distinctions reflected only outward appearances. Those who paid attention to the actual substance of Augustus' life and career, Tacitus claimed, had come to very different conclusions. They had not forgotten how the man later called Augustus had displayed no scruples in switching sides in the political battles of his youth. They recalled how – without any kind of official authorization – he had recruited soldiers with bribes, and had obtained his first government post on false pretenses, by feigning to favor the republican cause. His true distinguishing qualities had consisted of betrayal, duplicity toward his political opponents, and brutality toward ordinary citizens, whenever such means served the cause of his relentless striving for power. In the end he had overcome everyone – including Mark Antony and Aemilius Lepidus, his allies in the effort to bring down the republic – by means of deceit. Although peace prevailed afterwards, the cost in lives had been high both at home and abroad; countless Roman soldiers had died in addition to Augustus' political rivals. Only five years before Augustus' death the Romans had suffered enormous losses when the Germanic tribes inflicted a crushing defeat on Varus and his legions in what has traditionally been called "the battle of the Teutoburg Forest" (see below, page 102f.).

Tacitus' account reveals Augustus as a powerful and power-conscious leader – a far cry from the idealized figure of official pronouncements, whose political goals were supposedly determined solely by concern for the welfare of the Roman people. Indeed, the man who emerged from Tacitus' history was in many respects morally repellent, if one were only willing to look beneath the veneer of lofty phrases.

Both critics and loyal partisans agreed, however, that Augustus had been the driving force behind events in Rome for the fifty-eight years prior to his death. Following Caesar's death in 44 BC, he had suddenly entered public life and never again left the political stage. After 30 BC no opponent came forward who could have offered a serious challenge to his hold on power. From that point on Augustus dominated Rome and the empire, both politically and culturally. When he died it was clear to his detractors as well as supporters that the Roman state could no longer survive without the formal structure of monarchical rule that Augustus had introduced. Any attempt to demolish it would have meant civil war, a conflict that could easily have destroyed Rome's position as the dominant power in the Mediterranean, with no guarantee that the monarchy would not re-emerge at the end of it. As a result, almost everyone was willing to accept the status quo. The path to the creation of the monarchy had been long, and filled with casualties, experiments, and compromises. Paradoxically, so much suffering and uncertainty in the recent past helped to assure the permanence of the new form of rule.

2
Modest Origins, Powerful Relatives

The family of the man who would acquire the title *Augustus* came from Velitrae, a town about twenty miles southeast of Rome at the foot of the Alban Hills. His father, Gaius Octavius, had been born there as a knight, a member of the equestrian order that ranked second in Roman society below the order of senators. Like many other men from leading families in Italian towns in this period, he succeeded in joining the Senate, thereby obtaining entry into the governing class. After serving as *praetor*, Gaius Octavius became governor of Macedonia in the year 61 BC; he led a successful campaign against the Bessi, a Thracian tribe, and received the title of *imperator* by acclamation for his victory. This success would have enabled him to enter Rome in a triumphal procession and become a candidate for consul. He had got only as far as Nola, in Campania, on his way home, however, when he died, so that he never did join the inner circle of the Roman nobility, namely the group of senators who had served as consul and their families. As it turned out, this circumstance restricted the future prospects of his children less than it might have otherwise, since some time before 70 BC Gaius Octavius had taken as his second wife a woman named Atia. The marriage would have far-reaching consequences for the couple's offspring, for through her mother, Julia, Atia was the niece of Julius Caesar. Thus even though Gaius Octavius himself had never served as consul, he was connected with an old Roman family of patrician rank. (Patricians were descended from the families who had alone been able to exercise political power in the early republic.) At the time of Gaius Octavius' marriage the family of his in-laws had not played a leading role in politics for some time, but in the tradition-conscious society of Rome the relationship represented capital on which the family could draw at any time. As it happened, the connection proved decisive in the life of the couple's only son. Without it the history of Rome would have taken a different course as well; at least no Augustus would have arisen to shape its destiny.

This child, the second and last of Gaius Octavius and Atia's marriage, was born on September 23 in the year 63 BC and named after his father. The elder Gaius Octavius died four years later, and shortly thereafter his widow married Lucius Marcius Philippus, who became consul in 56 BC. This connection would prove useful to his stepson, but the dominant influence by far in the boy's life was his great-uncle Julius Caesar. Caesar was childless, and his closest male relatives were three great-nephews: Lucius Pinarius, Quintus Pedius, and the young Gaius Octavius. Like all Romans of rank, Caesar thought in terms that could be called dynastic, meaning that he intended the rank and privileges he attained to be passed on within his own family. Later Augustus acted on exactly the same principles.

No record has survived indicating that Julius Caesar had made specific plans for his great-nephew, and presumably the dictator died before he had even formed them clearly in his own mind. We know only that he had adopted the young Gaius Octavius and named him in his will as his principal heir, who would receive three-quarters of his estate. The other two great-nephews were to receive only one quarter between them both. It was understood that Octavian's acceptance of the large inheritance would go hand in hand with responsibility for certain payments also stipulated in the will. Caesar intended this money to go to the veterans from his military campaigns, as it was to this group of Roman citizens that he owed his political prominence. Although he did not spell out his intentions, Caesar certainly had some future role for his adopted son in view when he made the unequal provisions in his will. It was drawn up on 13 September 45 BC, at a point when it had already become clear that Caesar would not relinquish the power he had gained during the civil wars. He could not name a successor directly, however, without violating certain rules of the Republic that were still formally in force, and he probably also assumed that he had plenty of time left to make explicit provisions for the period after his death. Nonetheless the terms of Caesar's will, along with the elevation of his young relative to patrician rank and the public honors conferred on him, reveal his general intentions for the political succession clearly enough. Certainly neither Julius Caesar nor Octavius suspected how quickly the terms of his will would become relevant.

3
Seizing Power and Legalizing Usurpation

When Julius Caesar was murdered on 15 March 44 BC by his republican opponents, Octavius was away in Macedonia, in the town of Apollonia. He had gone there to complete his education, but was also expecting his great-uncle to arrive and take him along on a campaign against the Parthians. Caesar had already sent a number of legions to Macedonia in preparation for the expedition. When the news of Caesar's death reached Apollonia, some of Octavius' companions allegedly urged him to seize the opportunity and assume command of the troops. If these reports are true, then the young man must have rejected the step as too hasty, given his uncertain position at the time. As things stood he did not even know the provisions of Caesar's will. He did not learn what they were until he returned to Italy, and only then did he decide to become his great-uncle's political heir as well as heir to his estate. By then Octavius had grasped the message conveyed by the will.

Caesar's closest advisers came to Brundisium to confer with him. It is reported that the troops who had assembled there to sail with Caesar to fight the Parthians greeted the young heir enthusiastically. With this backing, Octavius took his first independent steps into politics. He demanded a portion of the funds that had been set aside for the Parthian campaign, and at the same time he appropriated the annual tribute from the province of Asia that had just arrived in Italy – without any entitlement or official mandate whatsoever. When Augustus later stated in his autobiographical account that, acting on his own initiative and at his own expense, he had raised an army to liberate the state from the threat of rule by faction, i.e. Antony, he reported the truth, but combined it with falsehood. The decision to seize Julius Caesar's political legacy by military force was indeed his own. If he had depended on his own financial resources, however, the attempt would soon have ended in failure.

With the money he had appropriated Octavius succeeded in winning over some of Caesar's veterans in Campania on his march to Rome. On May 6 he reached the capital and accepted Caesar's legacy, including his name. From then on he called himself Gaius Julius Caesar. The additional appellation *Octavianus*, which would have been customary in a case of adoption such as his own, was never used by Octavius himself, for it would have pointed too clearly to his modest origins. Nevertheless, in discussing the period of his life before he acquired the title *Augustus*, historians have traditionally referred to him as "Octavian" to distinguish him from his great-uncle Julius Caesar.

In the immediate wake of Caesar's assassination it was unclear which political faction would prevail. A general amnesty was proclaimed for Caesar's killers on March 17, but at the same time all the arrangements he had decided upon before his death were recognized. The two consuls were Mark Antony, one of Caesar's closest associates and Octavian's senior by almost twenty years, and Gnaeus Dolabella. By delivering his inflammatory eulogy at Caesar's funeral, Antony stirred up public unrest and succeeded in driving the assassins out of Rome. Nevertheless, he was by no means universally accepted as the leader of Caesar's party. It was probably these circumstances that led him to veer back and forth between the various political groups for an extended period, without making it clear where his loyalties lay. He lost favor with the plebs and the veterans, and also with some members of Caesar's party, since at first he opposed Caesar's elevation to the status of a god, an honor which a large number of Romans favored. Antony also went too far in trying to strengthen his own position by arranging for passage of the law that transferred to him the provinces of Gallia Cisalpina in northern Italy and Gallia Comata, the Gaul that Caesar had conquered. This step brought him into conflict with others in the Caesarian party. Of course Antony could not have anticipated that his strategy would help the man who was ultimately to become his nemesis to enter politics.

In Rome the young Caesar quickly gained more supporters. First he announced that he intended to avenge the murder of his adopted father, an aim that all recognized as legitimate, since his filial duty (*pietas*) required it. He demonstrated *pietas* as well in paying the sum of 300 sesterces to each member of the urban plebs, as stipulated in Caesar's will, after Antony had failed to carry out this instruction. Octavian also celebrated the games scheduled for late July to honor Caesar's victories, because the priests officially in charge of them hung back. When a comet (*sidus Iulium*) appeared during the games, it was declared a sign that Caesar should be made a god. Octavian demonstratively added an image of the comet to his father's statues. In this way he gained considerable popularity, which in turn became a factor in politics.

At the same time Octavian also negotiated, reaching an understanding with the moderates in Caesar's party, and even sending out feelers to some of the republicans. Antony endeavored to block the political rise of "the boy" – the polemical term he used to describe Octavian – but with only partial success. To be sure, Octavian's first march on Rome in the late autumn of 44, with veterans from Campania, failed to reach its objective. The soldiers, who sympathized with Caesar's

party, were not willing – yet – to fight other troops support-
ing the same faction. But the attempt made Antony so nervous
that he decided to leave Rome. He summoned the four
legions encamped near Brundisium, so that he could take over
the two provinces of Gaul early, before the term of Decimus
Brutus, the proconsul then in office, expired. But two of
Antony's legions, finding Octavian's money more attractive
than the orders of the legitimate consul, turned against him
and went over to his rival. Antony's withdrawal from Rome
began to look more like flight.

For his part, Octavian had little choice but to appeal to his
obligations as Caesar's son, since he had no official position
that would give him a legal basis on which to act. But then
the new political constellation provided him – not yet twenty
years of age – with the maneuvering room he needed.
Although the Caesarian party held a majority in the Senate,
the republicans prevailed, led by Cicero, the 62-year-old
former consul. Cicero succeeded because Antony's naked
power politics had inspired fear in many Caesarian senators.
But while the majority in the Senate could pass resolutions,
they could not force Antony to accept them, because they had
no soldiers. The Senate's need provided Octavian with his
opportunity, and he seized it. He did have troops, and he
placed them at the disposal of the Senate majority, who recip-
rocated by giving him an official position. The broker of this
alliance was Cicero. (Octavian realized that accepting the
Senate's offer to proceed against Antony would make it appear
for the moment as if he had forgotten his declared mission –
to avenge Caesar's death. He took the risk, however; for a
while he was even willing to collaborate with Caesar's
assassins.) Although Octavian had never held office before,
the Senate now made him a member and permitted him to
vote with the highest rank, the former consuls. In addition he
received a command (*imperium*), and a commission to march
against Antony.

Octavian took over the *fasces*, the symbols of command, for the first time on January 7, 43 BC; later he heightened the date's importance with a sacrifice, to present it as the start of a new era. For its part the Senate approved payment of the bonuses Octavian had promised to his soldiers. How Caesar's son presented this seeming political about-face to his troops is not clear, but he must have persuaded them to accept it, for they continued to follow him.

Octavian marched his army to Mutina in northern Italy, where Antony was besieging Decimus Brutus. The two consuls for the year 43 BC, Hirtius and Pansa, who both belonged to Caesar's party, also traveled north. In the decisive battle near Mutina on April 21, Antony was defeated, but both consuls had lost their lives in the fighting. Octavian took over their armies as if it were the most natural thing in the world, thereby increasing his military strength enormously. But the constellation of political power was shifting rapidly as well.

For one thing, while Octavian was conducting his campaign against Antony, the majority in the Senate gave legal recognition to the positions of power which Brutus and Cassius, the two leaders of the conspiracy against Caesar, had established for themselves. (Brutus had illegally occupied Macedonia and Cassius had done the same in Syria – both acting "on their own initiative," as Augustus would later characterize his own actions in the *Res Gestae*.) This was a serious setback for Octavian, as he no longer represented the sole military arm of the Senate. Some people, summing up the situation in very drastic terms, said that he should be "withdrawn from circulation." And secondly Antony, after fleeing from northern Italy to Gaul, was able to win over several governors in the West to his cause: Asinius Pollio, Munatius Plancus, and Aemilius Lepidus. They now proclaimed vengeance for Caesar's murder as their common political goal. To achieve it the Caesarian party would have to be united. It was clear to Octavian, in terms of both ideology and power politics, for which side he had to declare, if he wanted to go on playing a role. Nonetheless he first attempted to improve his own position.

Because both consuls had fallen in the fighting at Mutina, a delegation of centurions from Octavian's army marched to Rome demanding that the Senate name their commander as consul, and that the soldiers receive the bonuses promised earlier. When the senators refused, mistakenly believing that the balance of power lay with them, Octavian marched on Rome again. This time he was successful: Together with his uncle Quintus Pedius, as he stressed in the *Res Gestae*, he was formally elected consul by the people on August 19, 43 BC. But since after the Senate's refusal to meet their demands the centurions had returned to Rome accompanied by their legions, the people really had no choice at all. Octavian then had a law passed to create a special tribunal for Caesar's assassins, thereby giving concrete form to his much advertised duty to avenge Caesar's death. In addition he used funds from the state treasury to pay the veterans the money still owed them under the terms of Caesar's will. Now danger threatened from the north, from the coalition of Caesarians backing Antony. With wise foresight Octavian had the Senate rescind the decree that had declared Antony and his followers enemies of the state. This tactical move made it easier to conduct the negotiations that followed next.

4

The Triumvirate: Dictatorship Sanctioned by Law

Antony, Octavian, and Lepidus met near Bologna in October to make plans for the future. Taking vengeance on the murderers of Caesar and securing their own position of power were their main goals. They came to no agreement about restructuring the government, even though the titles they adopted might suggest that they had. They chose to call themselves *tresviri rei publicae constituendae*, a triumvirate for constituting the state. Whereas the agreement once reached by Pompey, Julius Caesar, and Crassus had been a purely private one, the three men now arranged for the assembly of the plebs to validate their pact by giving them an official mandate. Although virtual dictators, they were determined not to be outdone by their republican opponents in preserving the outward form of legality if they could do so without jeopardizing their own interests. A plebiscite on November 27, 43 BC, provided them with offices and titles. Their mandate was limited to five years, but virtually unlimited in terms of power. Any decision they made would have the force of law, and no one could legally prevent it from taking effect. As a result, the plebiscite made violent resistance the only form of opposition to triumvirs. That did not bode well for the future.

Fears about the triumvirs' intentions proved to be justified. They began by dividing the western part of the empire among themselves: Lepidus received the provinces of Gallia Narbonensis and Spain, while Octavian's share was Sicily, Sardinia, and Africa. Antony retained Gallia Cisalpina and Gallia Comata, however, as had been determined previously by plebiscite. This put him in the strongest position in military terms, while weakening Octavian considerably. The two islands were of little use to him as long as Sextus Pompeius, the surviving son of Pompey the great, controlled the seas with his fleet. And if Octavian wanted to control Africa in practice as well as theory, he would have to conquer it first.

The next part of the plan was for Antony and Octavian to take up the fight against Caesar's assassins together. To carry it out their principal need was for money to keep the troops motivated. They also needed to make sure that their opponents in Italy and Rome could not seize power behind their backs while they were fighting in the East. The tactics for preventing this – proscriptions – had been devised by Sulla, who had also introduced Romans to civil war as a political strategy in 88 BC. The triumvirs followed Sulla's brutal model. They declared their political opponents to be outlaws; anyone was free to kill them, and in order to interest as many people as possible in the manhunt, they also offered rewards. When someone was caught and killed, his assets were seized and sold, with the profits going to the triumvirs. They entered the names of about 300 senators and 2,000 knights in the proscription lists. Octavian reportedly resisted adopting this procedure for several days, chiefly because he wanted to save Cicero. But Antony hated Cicero passionately, and Octavian's efforts were in vain. But even if Octavian's reluctance in Cicero's case was genuine and credible, his associates did not have to force brutal measures on him in general. He demonstrated his own cruelty clearly enough in chilling examples over the following years. Only later did Octavian come to recognize *clementia Caesaris* – the clemency practiced by his adoptive father, Julius Caesar – as a political virtue.

The proscriptions decimated the leading senatorial class appallingly. Many families belonging to the republican core of the Senate were completely wiped out, and the triumvirs were then able to fill the gaps with their own people. They achieved a similar effect by murdering wealthy members of city councils. Loyal supporters from the army replaced the assassinated councillors in large numbers, and often took over their property as well. These and other measures led to a far-reaching shift in leadership – Ronald Syme, one of the great Roman historians of the twentieth century, called it the "Roman revolution." Even though the structure of society remained essentially unchanged, republican traditions were so weakened that they could be replaced by something new. The proscriptions and murders brought about a radical reorientation of loyalties in political bodies, establishing a foundation on which the Augustan form of rule could later be erected.

In this sense the proscriptions were successful, but the financial gain for which the triumvirs had hoped failed to materialize. They were thus forced into the position of having to impose special taxes in order to wage civil war. In the East, Brutus and Cassius had squeezed the money they needed out of the population there and created nineteen legions; in addition they could call on local rulers to provide further troops for support. They gathered their forces in Macedonia, and Antony and Octavian sent 28 legions there by sea. Since the republican fleet dominated the Adriatic Sea and blocked a retreat to Italy, the triumvirs needed a rapid and decisive battle on land.

In October of 42 BC the fateful meeting at Philippi took place. The armies of Caesar's assassins and the triumvirs met twice, and both times the actual victor was Antony. When Antony and Octavian later became enemies, Antony made polemical attacks in which he presented Octavian as a coward who had fled at the sight of the foe. It seems to be true that such engagements overtaxed him; later Octavian left direct military command to other, more seasoned soldiers such as Marcus Agrippa. What counted, however, was victory; after October 42 the republicans had no army and no leaders left. Brutus and Cassius were dead; according to the Roman biographer and historian Suetonius (*Life of Augustus*, 13, 1) the victors placed Brutus' head on display in Rome. They could now set about dividing the Roman world anew.

Antony retained his command over Gaul (giving him a strong position), but was now supposed to go to the East, to pacify the region and raise money to pay the veterans. His assignment appeared to pose no great problems. Octavian received the Spanish provinces as a power base, conceded to him by Antony at Lepidus' expense. But the young Caesar's next task was a far more thankless one: to find a place to settle the veterans – the tens of thousands of soldiers whom the triumvirs had promised to discharge as soon as the battle at Philippi was won. If this were not enough, they also had to settle the soldiers who had fought on the republican side; they could not be permitted to roam the world at will looking for an ambitious politician to hire them. At that time Italy itself, the homeland of Roman citizens, still seemed almost the only place where veterans' settlements could be founded. More land would have been available in the provinces, but that was not yet a widely accepted option. The problem was that no more state-owned land existed in Italy; if Octavian wanted to make room for veterans there, the land would have to be confiscated. Confiscation, in turn, cost a high price politically, for in their anger the citizens evicted from their property would rally behind virtually any political opponent of the men who had driven them out. Octavian must have realized this, yet he took on the mandate which – at least in hindsight – provided an important foundation for his ultimate victory. By creating settlements for the veterans he gained a broad clientele that thought in military terms, and also a far stronger political following in Italy, the core domain of Roman power.

At least 18 Italian towns were affected by the new settlements; in some of them the entire population was dispossessed and driven out, while in others the evictions were partial. A tide of fury swept the country. Only rarely were exceptions granted, as in the case of Virgil, who was allowed to keep his inherited estates near Mantua. He expressed his gratitude in one of his *Eclogues*, but the majority of inhabitants in the affected towns cursed Octavian. This did not alter the fact that they were powerless to stop the settlements.

As the confiscations proceeded Octavian's assignment put his life in danger, for the dispossessed found a leader in Lucius Antonius, brother of the triumvir. The extent to which Mark Antony participated in his actions is now difficult to determine, but Lucius Antonius – with or without his brother's direct assistance – succeeded in gathering a coalition against Octavian in Italy, supported by the majority in the Senate. Once Mark Antony began concentrating his operations in the distant East, he had ceased to appear so dangerous to the senators, who now saw Octavian as the more serious threat. Even members of the Caesarian party, his own allies, had become aware of his unscrupulousness. They tried to have the triumvirate declared illegal and Octavian an enemy of the state. The problem was that the veterans and soldiers still on active duty depended on the triumvirs for their financial security and political recognition of their interests. Dissolving the triumvirate would have alienated a more dangerous group than the dispossessed property owners. And so in the end Octavian and his military following prevailed over Lucius Antonius, whose political gamble ended in disaster. Lucius Antonius had withdrawn with his supporters, including many senators, to the strongly fortified town of Perusia (modern Perugia) on the border of Etruria and Umbria. Octavian laid siege to the town and finally forced it to surrender early in 40 BC. He spared

Lucius Antonius out of consideration for his powerful brother in the East, but he had the citizens of Perusia massacred, and showed no mercy to the Roman senators and knights who had sought safety in the town. It is reported that he gave orders for 300 of them to be executed on March 15, the anniversary of Caesar's assassination, at an altar to the deified Julius Caesar outside the walls of the town. Octavian bore the onus of this butchery for a long time; the Augustan poet Propertius is only one of the writers who condemned the triumvir and lamented the victims.

In the short term, the victory created only a little relief. Many of Antony's followers whom Octavian had spared at Perusia fled to the East, hoping to persuade Antony to intervene in Italy. Antony turned his attention westward, even though the Parthians had achieved alarming successes in Syria and Asia Minor, in order to face the greater threat to his political position at home. Octavian was operating in Italy as if he were in sole command. An opportunity presented itself to Antony to join forces with Sextus Pompeius, who controlled the western Mediterranean, with the aim of eliminating Octavian as a rival for power. Thus we find Antony, a leading member of the Caesarian party, in a virtual alliance with a supporter of the republican faction; in politics, a chance of victory justified almost anything. Where a lack of scruples was concerned, however, Octavian did not lag far behind Antony. Octavian made his own attempt to create ties to Sextus Pompeius by marrying a woman from a family close to him in the year 40; his bride, Scribonia, was the daughter of Scribonius Libo, a follower of Sextus Pompeius and also his father-in-law. This marriage, which lasted little more than a year, produced Octavian's only child, his daughter Julia. Julia would play an important role in politics later on, but one that ended in personal tragedy for her.

Antony returned to Italy with a large force, but his arrival did not bring about a military solution. He laid siege to

Brundisium, which was occupied by the troops of his rival. Once again, however, the legions committed to the Caesarian cause refused to fight, following their centurions. The centurions had become important figures politically, largely because they could influence the men under their command. The two leaders were compelled to seek an agreement. In the autumn of 40 BC Octavian and Antony approved the treaty of Brundisium, which ultimately proved a great success for Octavian. He lost Africa, which was given to Lepidus, but otherwise gained all the western provinces, while Antony retained the eastern ones. A special provision declared that Italy was to be open to all for the purpose of recruiting soldiers. The fact that Antony claimed recruiting rights suggests he recognized what was at stake. He returned to the East, however, leaving Octavian in Italy by himself, so that in practice the treaty's provision was of no use to him. After concluding the treaty, the two rivals cemented their negotiations with a wedding in a typically dynastic fashion; Antony, whose wife had died not long before, married Octavia, Octavian's sister, in a splendid ceremony in Rome. Her fate and that of her children, both from her previous marriage to Claudius Marcellus and her union with Antony, remained closely linked to the political fortunes of her brother. What role Octavia played in the struggle between her brother and husband – whether chiefly that of mediator or victim – it is difficult to determine.

5
The Path to Formal Legitimation as a Ruler

The treaty of Brundisium did not bring peace to Italy – even though the poet Virgil announced the dawn of a golden age in his fourth *Eclogue* – for Sextus Pompeius continued to control the seas, threatening Italy and hindering the import of grain. He took to calling himself *Neptuni filius*, "son of Neptune," for good reason. Rome and many other cities and towns throughout Italy were affected by the grain shortage. The pressure on Octavian to come to terms with this opponent grew so strong that finally, in 39 BC, he reluctantly concluded the treaty of Misenum. By its terms he granted official recognition to Pompeius as a competitor for power, and conceded to him a territorial base consisting of Sardinia, Corsica, Sicily, and the Peloponnese. Octavian also promised the consulship for the year 35 to Pompeius, in what appeared to represent a decisive step toward reconciliation and the restoration of peace. For his part, Pompeius agreed to lift the blockade of Italy and ended the attacks by his vessels, ensuring that the people there would once again receive adequate supplies of grain. The inclusion of Pompeius' supporters in the treaty of Misenum enabled some of them, who had either escaped the proscriptions or fled during the civil wars, to return home and re-enter public life. This group included

Tiberius Claudius Nero, a member of an old patrician family, and his wife, Livia Drusilla, who belonged to a branch of the Claudian family herself. She was the granddaughter of M. Livius Drusus, who had labored to integrate the Italic population into the Roman political community in 91 BC, and the daughter of a senator. Since the leading families of Rome tended to think in genealogical and dynastic terms, the effect Livia could have on uniting different clans was enormous.

Octavian certainly did not overlook this circumstance when he attempted to win her from her husband after they returned to Rome. But political calculations alone do not explain why Octavian was in such a hurry to marry Livia – he was passionately in love with her. She was then pregnant, a circumstance that normally made divorce and immediate remarriage to another man impossible. However, Octavian obtained special permission from the college of priests to marry Livia, and the ceremony took place on January 17 in 38 BC. In Rome tongues wagged about the scandal. Three months after the wedding she gave birth to a second son, Drusus; her firstborn, Tiberius, was then four years old. Both boys joined their mother in Octavian's house after their father died; Nero had named him as the boys' guardian in his will. Perhaps Nero sensed that such a close link with Octavian represented the best possible improvement of their political prospects, but it could never have entered his mind that 52 years later his elder son would become ruler of the Roman Empire. The path to that rank, at the side of Octavian, the later Augustus, would be long, and filled with both honors and humiliations.

Octavian's marriage to Livia strengthened his base in the old aristocracy, but did not prevent him from quickly repudiating the treaty of Misenum. Its official recognition of Pompeius' power hemmed Octavian in too much, for in contrast to Antony, who was occupied with matters in the East, Pompeius remained too close to make a comfortable ally. And so Octavian tried to break his opponent's hold on his power base before the year 38 BC was out. One of Pompeius' naval commanders was willing to betray his master, and handed over Corsica and Sardinia to Octavian. But Pompeius was too strong to be beaten quickly, and Octavian could not count on Antony's support. Antony had no wish to see Pompeius defeated, for he was an effective brake on the fierce ambition of his colleague in the triumvirate. Octavian thus had two tasks: first to build up his own fleet into an effective fighting force, and secondly to gain both Antony's consent and cooperation for an attack on Pompeius. The task of building up the fleet fell to Agrippa, who used new methods to train the sailors for battle. And Antony gave his consent largely because he needed Octavian's cooperation for the difficult situation he was facing in the East. Antony had succeeded in stopping the Parthians' advance, but had not yet taken revenge on them for the crushing defeat they had inflicted on Crassus at the battle of Carrhae in 53 BC. The public was impatient for him to fulfill his promise to restore the honor of Rome; politically, he could not afford to make people wait too long. In addition Antony wanted to extend his power beyond the existing eastern frontier, perhaps under the influence of Queen Cleopatra of Egypt. This had been Julius Caesar's goal as well. But for such an undertaking Antony needed experienced troops, whom he could recruit only in Italy, now effectively the power base of Octavian. The two leaders therefore had to meet for negotiations, which took place in the town of Tarentum on the southern coast of Italy. Even though each wanted an important concession from the other, the negotiations proved difficult, and it took Octavia's diplomatic intervention for the parties to achieve a successful balance of interests. They also had to reach agreement about how to continue the triumvirate, for it had expired on December 31, 38 BC.

In September 37 they arranged to extend the triumvirate for another five years, although it remains unclear today whether they declared this term to have begun retroactively on January 1, 37, or dated it from January 1, 36. While the official dates remained unimportant compared with the real distribution of power, it would be useful to know precisely what the arrangements were, for that would shed light on the triumvirs' attitude toward their legal position and the institutions of the state. However, the surviving sources do not reveal the details, although more speaks for the year 37. It is noteworthy that Octavian had the extension of the triumvirate formally ratified by the assembly of the plebs, and thereafter referred to himself as "triumvir for the second time" (*triumvir rei publicae constituendae iterum*). The ratification was intended to signal to the public, and in particular to the Senate, that he respected the legal norms and regarded himself as a part of the *res publica*, and not above it. Antony dispensed with such legal niceties. Lepidus, whose participation had led to the creation of a triumvirate in the first place, clearly played no further role at the time of its renewal.

The mutual aid pact achieved by the negotiations called for Antony to provide 120 ships to Octavian for use against Sextus Pompeius, while Octavian was to send 20,000 legionaries to Antony for the Parthian campaign. Antony made the ships available immediately, and so the conference at Tarentum, the last time Octavian and Antony met face to face, ended on a friendly note. Later, however, Octavian sent only one-tenth of the troops he had promised to Antony – as an intentional provocation. When they ran up against one another six years later, it was as enemies at the battle of Actium, an encounter that spelled the beginning of the end for Antony.

All that lay in the future, however; in the meantime Caesar's first concern was to remove Pompeius as a threat. To accomplish this aim he had to continue the civil war, a move he later tried to cover up in the *Res Gestae* by referring to it as a "war against pirates." It is unlikely that many people took that view of the campaign in the year 36. Octavian chose Sicily as the base of operations for his army and navy, and Lepidus sailed from Africa with his legions to meet him, in the third triumvir's last intervention in the general struggle for power. After various setbacks, in which Octavian's own life was at risk, Agrippa met Pompeius off the Sicilian coast at the naval battles of Mylai (in August 36) and Naulochos (on September 3, 36), defeating him so thoroughly that Pompeius fled with his fleet to the East. There he continued to cause Antony problems for a while. Then in 35 BC he fell into the hands of one of Antony's generals, who had him executed in Miletus. Some units of Pompeius' army on Sicily surrendered to Octavian, and others to Lepidus. As a result the latter felt greatly empowered and demanded control over the whole island. He had overestimated his own strength, however, and not reckoned with his opponent's skill in influencing the troops, despite the fact that Octavian had demonstrated his ability to sway large masses of people many times since May of 44. His psychological skills were usually connected with promises of money, so that his hearers did not find it all that difficult to change sides. And so it happened now. Lepidus' troops defected to his erstwhile ally, and their commander had no alternative but to surrender. This saved his life, but of course Lepidus had to resign his position as triumvir. Octavian confined him under guard in a villa at Cape Circei, halfway between Rome and Naples. The only office he was permitted to retain until his death in 12 BC was that of *pontifex maximus*, head of the college of priests. By leaving Lepidus as chief priest Octavian was making another display of his respect for Roman traditions; priests had always been appointed for life, and this custom had to be honored even in the case of one's worst enemy. Perhaps a few cynics noted that with Lepidus' resignation the triumvirate had effectively ceased to exist, but no one seemed to mind very much.

What may have mattered more was a gesture Octavian made at this time to the inhabitants of Italy to demonstrate that he respected certain social traditions, in particular the rights of property owners. Countless slaves had fled to Pompeius, who had allowed them to join his army and navy. When they were captured, Octavian returned more than 30,000 of them to their former owners directly, in recognition of the fact that only the slaves' owners had the right to destroy or devalue their own "property." In the case of the 6,000 whose former owners could not be traced, Octavian gave orders for all of them to be crucified without mercy. The free men among Pompeius' followers were offered pardons, however, in particular the officers. People understood these signals clearly, as well as the signals Octavian sent to the army. After Pompeius was defeated, soldiers with many years of service in Octavian's forces insisted that he fulfill the promises made to them long before. Octavian had to meet their demands for discharge from the army, and settlement on their own land. At this juncture he decided to settle the veterans outside Italy, an option for which there was limited precedent from the time of Julius Caesar. Italy could no longer take in all her rootless sons, for that would have meant perpetuating the dispossession of the propertied classes. Octavian wished to send a signal that citizens would no longer have to fear losing their land. He intended it to announce the start of a lasting peace. In reality, however, more than half a decade would pass before peace finally arrived.

On his return to Rome from Sicily Octavian was honored with a triumph as a victorious commander. This was possible because in the official version of events he had defeated the pirates. As tradition required, he waited outside the sacred city limits, the *pomerium*, for the members of the Senate to come out to meet him. After the victor had officially declared the civil wars to be over, it seemed that the Senate could not do enough to honor the man who was now sole ruler in the West. For his own future safety it was important to Octavian that he be awarded the immunity of a tribune, *sacrosanctitas*. In Roman political theory and practice the tribunes of the plebs, whose special task was to represent the interests and welfare of the people, had immunity from all forms of attack and prosecution. (The conferral of tribunicial immunity foreshadowed the ruler's later acquisition of the official powers of a tribune of the people, which from 23 BC on would provide Augustus with a crucial basis of political legality.) Soon afterwards Livia and Octavia were also granted immunity. By declaring them sacrosanct, the Senate and the people promised to grant special protection to Octavian and both women. Anyone who violated their immunity would be deemed to have committed a crime against the Roman people itself. It was the beginning of a process in which the ruling family would come to stand for and finally replace it altogether. But this, too, lay far ahead.

For the time being Antony had the entire East firmly in his grip, and had many supporters in Italy as well, not a few of whom were members of the Senate. Since he was far away, people tended not to hold him as responsible for the ruthlessness prevailing in politics, or for the sense of helplessness many felt. The political scene in Rome was largely dominated by the young Caesar, so he bore the brunt of Romans' anger and frustration, despite all the attempts he made to put politics back on a foundation in law. Among his most angry and frustrated opponents were the members of the old senatorial families. To increase the number of his supporters in the Senate, Octavian arranged for many new people to be voted into office as quaestors, tribunes of the plebs, aediles, and praetors. He recruited them from cities previously not represented in the Senate, and placed them in office; they were his puppets, and Octavian could depend on them for political support. Antony's absence prevented him from responding effectively. All Antony could count on was the distribution of consuls equally to the supporters of both sides, as required by the treaty of Brundisium. Octavian did not tamper with this arrangement, despite all his other attempts to reduce his adversary's influence.

Yet far from remaining passive, Antony even played into Octavian's hands at this point, although one should bear in mind that, as the ultimate victor, Octavian influenced the historical record both directly and indirectly. A number of reports concerning Antony, his actions, and his supporters are only half-truths or even complete fabrications. Nevertheless, Antony provided Octavian with enough weighty and compelling arguments to justify taking action against him. At the same time that Octavian defeated Pompeius in the West, Antony suffered a serious setback in his campaign against the Parthians. He achieved the exact opposite of what he had set out to do: Instead of winning military glory and recapturing the battle standards lost by Crassus, he suffered a humiliating defeat; instead of capturing territory and booty, he incurred catastrophic losses of troops and equipment. It took Antony time to find replacements for both, and this limited his capability to respond. Worst of all, however, he first sent back reports that he had won, to try to limit the immediate damage. His victory was even celebrated at home with ceremonies of thanksgiving. In the end, of course, news of his defeat reached Rome. It was a propaganda debacle, and the great commander's reputation was tarnished.

A further loss of prestige soon followed, orchestrated by Octavian. In a well-calculated act of provocation, he sent Octavia out to Antony accompanied by only 2,000 legionnaires instead of the 20,000 promised in the treaty of Tarentum. Antony faced a dilemma. The soldiers Octavian had provided did not make up for his earlier losses. The only other person in a position to make them good was Cleopatra, the queen of Egypt with whom Antony had a long-standing liaison, and several children. With the resources of Egypt at her disposal, Cleopatra could restore his army to full strength. But he could hardly count on her support if he allowed his wife to join him and remain with him in the East. A realistic appraisal of the military situation alone would have tipped the balance in Cleopatra's favor, for Antony urgently needed her money and troops, but he was also deeply in love with her. He ordered Octavia to return to Rome, thereby giving his brother-in-law the best possible grounds for a propaganda campaign against him: Antony had rejected Octavia, his legitimate spouse and a Roman, for an "Oriental paramour." Antony's republican supporters in the Senate could not come up with much in the way of a rebuttal, and such a juicy story made it easy for Octavian to stir up the masses against him. Then, in the year 34 BC, Roman troops conquered Armenia. When Antony made Alexander Helios, one of his sons by Cleopatra, king of that country and awarded the title "Queen of Kings" to Cleopatra herself, he gave Octavian enough ammunition to claim that his rival had diminished the pre-eminence and dignity of Rome, and to turn public opinion against him. It did not matter whether or not Antony might have had good reasons for his actions; Octavian chose to see them as a challenge. In addition, Antony formally recognized Julius Caesar as the father of Cleopatra's son Caesarion. This represented a provocation, because Octavian used appeals to the memory of the murdered Caesar as a unifying force in his party. He had taken Julius Caesar's name and stressed his status as *divi filius*, "son of the deified one," but everyone knew that he was a son only by adoption.

The provocations offered by both sides had one advantage: they solidified the enmity between the two parties and increased their willingness to force a final decision. Now it was only a question of who would declare war first. The propagandists had already opened the hostilities.

6
The Final Battles for Power:
Actium and Alexandria

On January 1 of the year 33 BC Octavian became consul again. He opened the first session of the Senate with a vehement attack on Antony's grants of territory and titles in the East, accusing him of betraying Roman interests. When Antony heard of this on his march toward Armenia, he broke off the campaign against the Parthians. Fearing that Octavian might form his own conspiracy against him with foreign enemies – and possibly even attempt to recruit some of the rulers of his and Cleopatra's satellite kingdoms – Antony decided to take the initiative. He ordered his army and navy to assemble at Ephesus on the coast of Asia Minor, and summoned forces from Egypt and its dependent dynasties. Octavian prevented Antony from gaining any access to Italy, although the treaty of Tarentum had guaranteed both rulers a free hand to recruit soldiers there. A treaty meant little, however, when supreme power was at stake. If Antony would not be fobbed off with the status of an Eastern potentate and insisted on a continuing role in Rome, then he would have to back up his claims with force.

Octavian had been preparing for a military confrontation for some time himself. In effect he treated the campaign in Illyricum from 35 to 33 BC as an exercise for his troops that would also provide him with an opportunity to demonstrate – and then publicize – his skill as a military commander. In the past Antony had often accused him of cowardice, so Octavian could even make use of a wound he incurred as part of a propaganda campaign to improve his image. The fleet remained under the command of Agrippa, who continued to build it up; it appeared not unlikely that the decisive battle would take place at sea. In addition both he and Octavian wanted to make their naval forces strong enough to prevent Antony from crossing the Adriatic and making a successful landing in Italy. They were determined that the homeland would not become a theater of war again.

Even though Antony was gathering his forces in the year 33, the official break did not take place until the following year. Perhaps Antony was still hoping to improve his military position, and also to make gains on the propaganda front, since two of his closest allies, Gaius Sosius and Domitius Ahenobarbus, were to become consuls on January 1 of 32 BC. Furthermore, it is possible that he was waiting for the triumvirate to expire at the end of 33. For Antony himself, who was so far away, this had little meaning, but in Rome and throughout Italy, where decisions voted by the Roman people had to be taken more seriously, formal expiration of their term of office might create difficulties for his rivals. While such problems were not insurmountable, they might give Antony a tactical advantage. Seizing his opportunity, Sosius delivered a polemic against the absent Octavian in the opening session of the Senate on January 1. He made such a deep impression on the senators that Octavian felt an aggressive response was necessary. He appeared at the next session with armed supporters – a clearer signal than his previous verbal attacks on Antony for betraying Roman interests in the East. As yet Octavian had no proof yet for these accusations; all he could do was announce that they would be produced in the following session. Nevertheless the two consuls, still nominally the highest magistrates in Rome, left the city in haste and fled to Antony, accompanied by more than 300 senators, many from old families and supporters of the republic. Although Antony ruled the East in the same autocratic spirit and was linked with an Oriental queen to boot, he still seemed to them more tolerable as a leader than Octavian, for all his traditional Roman demeanor. Romans had experienced his coldly calculated striving for power and learned to fear or despise him. Antony, on the other hand, was far away, so many people dismissed negative reports about him as propaganda. Some of those who fled Rome quickly came to recognize their error in having believed Antony to be in any real way superior to Octavian, but by then it was too late; they had already defected.

For the time being, the backing of so many prominent senators raised Antony's standing greatly. The fact that he was now backed by a rump Senate, in a manner of speaking, added to the legitimacy of his position; he denounced his opponent for suppressing republican freedom, which had in essence consisted of freedom of speech for senators. In the modern era Octavian's use of armed supporters to intimidate the members of the Senate has been described as a coup d'état. This assessment is not unproblematic, as we do not know for certain that the triumvirate's term of office had expired. And since Antony continued to refer to himself as triumvir, his legal situation was no better than Octavian's. In the last analysis both regarded legal considerations as ammunition in the political struggle for power, where winning was all that counted.

Octavian acquired the proof he had promised to show the Senate in the aftermath of so many senators' flight to Antony. When they arrived in the East, they discovered the triumvir in the company of Cleopatra, who had sailed with him to Athens from Ephesus. The pair were surrounded with all the splendor of a Hellenistic court. Here at last she prevailed upon the man she considered her husband to divorce Octavia. Whether she and Antony ever married in an official ceremony is not known. For a marriage to be valid by Roman standards, the rump Senate in Athens would have had to grant him a special waiver, and it is unlikely that they did so, for tensions were mounting between the queen and the Romans in Antony's entourage. They observed the influence of their leader's consort on political and military decisions. They found Octavian's claims that the gods of Egypt had declared war on the Romans' Jupiter personified in Cleopatra, so to speak. What would this mean for Rome, and also for the senators' own status as leaders of the Roman government? Many senators must have reacted with a mix of rational calculations and deep-rooted emotions. Antony refused to recognize how dangerous the situation was becoming for him, and that he was playing into his opponent's hands. At the very least he ought to have realized it when Munatius Plancus and his nephew Marcus Titius, loyal supporters of his for almost a decade, went over to Octavian in the autumn of 32 BC. But Antony either failed to recognize what was happening or could not muster the determination to act. It gave the advantage to Octavian.

The defectors brought Octavian the information he needed to confirm the accusations he had raised against Antony. Munatius Plancus knew the contents of Antony's last will and testament, for he had witnessed and signed it. He also knew that the original document had been deposited for safe keeping with the Vestal Virgins in Rome. In his will, Plancus told Octavian, Antony had left instructions that he should be buried at Cleopatra's side in Alexandria; he had also willed territories to his children by the queen, which they were to rule as monarchs. Since the lands in question had been conquered by Roman armies, however, Romans viewed them as part of their own empire and not Antony's to dispose of. The triumvir's betrayal appeared to be confirmed, and his wish for a tomb in Alexandria proved that he had renounced his origins. In any event this is what Octavian and his propagandists declared.

Obtaining proof of Munatius Plancus' report meant so much to him that Octavian was even willing to take on himself the onus of invading the Vestals' sanctuary. Having forced the chief priestess to hand the document over to him, he read the relevant passages aloud in the Senate. He said he had shown the document to no one else, but that also meant no one was able to confirm Octavian's claims. To defend his shocking violation of the priestesses' sacred sphere Octavian appealed to emergency powers that could be invoked when the safety of Rome was threatened. The dispositions of the will, as they have come down to us, are probably authentic, although we may – and probably should – doubt whether Octavian revealed the full contents to the senators.

At long last Octavian could take official action. He induced the Senate to revoke all of Antony's powers, including his long-scheduled consulship for the year 31 BC. The senators declared war not against Antony but against Cleopatra, however, on the grounds that it was her troops that threatened Rome and Italy. Antony was declared to be completely infatuated with her; he had fallen under her spell and was incapable of action. By making this the official version of the situation, the senators avoided the necessity of declaring civil war, the form of conflict that had proved so damaging to Rome in the past. After his victory over Pompeius Octavian had announced the era of civil wars to be at an end, so another description had to be found. In reality, of course, no one was deceived about the character of the coming war. That made it all the more important for each leader to try to motivate as many followers as possible and broaden his support. In the *Res Gestae* Augustus claimed that he had all Italy behind him – using the famous phrase *consensus universorum*, "universal consensus" – and that the people demanded that he serve as their leader in the war. He presented himself as merely carrying out the will of Roman citizens, who swore an oath of loyalty to him, as did the inhabitants of the western provinces. But the oath was not taken as freely and spontaneously everywhere as later reports suggested. There were ways to make people come forward as "volunteers." Furthermore, the population of Italian cities included veterans by the tens of thousands, and the former centurions, now widely represented in city and town councils, sided with Caesar's son, to whom they owed their discharge payments. They knew who among their neighbors belonged to the opposition, and in many places succeeded in intimidating them. Now the fact that Octavian had earlier taken on the highly unpopular task of settling the veterans began to pay off for him, although many difficulties certainly remained. For welcome as declarations of loyalty and oaths were, Octavian also desperately needed money. The inhabitants of Italy were required to turn over one-quarter of their annual incomes to finance the campaign, causing rebellions to break out in a number of places. There were enough troops available to quell them, however, and the soldiers seized the money intended for them.

In Rome itself, Agrippa had served as aedile – a magistrate in charge of public works and public order who was elected annually – in 33 BC, and improved conditions for the plebs, thereby strengthening support for the Caesarian party. He had overseen the construction of two new aqueducts, the *Aqua Virgo* and *Aqua Iulia*, and the installation of new fountains throughout the city. Providing fresh water for drinking, for public baths, and for sewers that improved sanitary conditions in the city turned out to be no less important a means of influencing the plebs than keeping the city supplied with grain; these useful measures helped to procure support for Octavian's policies in other areas. In the conflict with Antony, he effectively exploited the theme of concern for the future welfare of the republic. Rome and Italy, ran the argument, were making a united front against the "attempt of a degenerate Roman to install a barbarian queen upon the Capitol with her eunuchs, her mosquito-nets and all the apparatus of oriental luxury."* By contrast, it was implied, Octavian's ties to Rome were indissoluble. It was to underscore this that at this time he began construction on a monumental tomb for himself on the Campus Martius, to offer as demonstrative and public a contrast as possible to Antony's desire to be buried in Alexandria. He staged the formal declaration of war against Cleopatra in a similarly public manner by officiating as priest (*fetialis*) in a revived rite that called for him to hurl a ritual lance into a square of ground in Rome symbolizing enemy territory. It was another bow to tradition.

Antony wanted the war to be fought in Italy – so that was precisely what Octavian had to prevent. Early in 31 BC Octavian and Agrippa scored a preliminary victory by success-fully ferrying their troops across the Adriatic. The bulk of the eastern forces' army and navy were assembled around the Gulf of Ambracia in northwestern Greece; smaller detach-ments were positioned to keep the crucial passages to Egypt open. Agrippa rapidly overpowered them, cutting off Antony and Cleopatra's main force from its supply routes. Meanwhile Octavian landed on the mainland opposite the island of Corcyra (present-day Corfu) and marched south. Soon both Antony's army and navy were trapped on land and at sea. All his attempts to engage Octavian in a land battle failed. Octavian could afford to wait while time worked for him. Soldiers from Antony's forces deserted daily, and many of the eastern kings, not all of whom had joined Cleopatra's coalition voluntarily, observed the situation tipping against them. They decided to look after their own interests and deserted from Antony's army as well. The attrition rate also rose among the naval crews, as the effects of Agrippa's blockade made them-selves felt and the summer heat brought outbreaks of disease.

* Ronald Syme, *The Roman Revolution* (1939; rpt. Oxford: Oxford University Press, 1960), 289.

By August Antony had at most half of his original troop strength remaining. The worst blow to his confidence, however, must have been the defection of Domitius Ahenobarbus, one of his chief supporters for many years. Ahenobarbus knew how much damage was being done to Antony's cause by Cleopatra's display of influence and her conspicuous participation in military and political decisions. When he realized that Antony would not change his attitude, Ahenobarbus decided to leave. Other senators followed his example, after a dispassionate or desperate calculation of the odds. Later, during the Augustan era, whether one had fought on the ruler's side at Actium would be a fact of some importance. Augustus himself stressed in the *Res Gestae* that at this time he had the support of more than 700 senators – including 83 who reached the highest office, the consulate – and about 170 members of the priestly colleges. Since only the most prominent Romans could achieve either status, Augustus wanted to make clear that everyone who counted in Rome had rallied around him patriotically.

The situation at Actium was growing worse for Antony by the day. If he waited any longer, his forces would be so weak that he would lose all strategic alternatives. Therefore he determined to seek an encounter as a means of fleeing – a decision that may seem paradoxical, but in fact made perfect sense. He did not intend to seek victory, as is evident from the fact that his ships carried large sails, which would only have been in the way in a pitched battle. Antony's actual goal was to break through the blockade and flee. On September 2 in 31 BC the two fleets, commanded by Gaius Sosius, who had been consul in the year 32 BC, and Agrippa, took up battle positions and waited. When the fighting finally began about midday, Agrippa's fleet and tactics proved superior. Although his ships were smaller, they outnumbered Antony's and were more maneuverable, so Agrippa was able to bottle up his opponent's large, unwieldy vessels. When it became clear to Cleopatra, waiting with her own fleet in the Gulf of Actium, that Antony was not breaking through the blockade as planned, she ordered her ships to hoist their sails and force their way through the middle of the battle. Antony followed her, and the outcome was decided. His legions capitulated as well, but only after negotiating favorable conditions with Octavian, including discharge bonuses. Such generosity on the part of the victor paid off both politically and militarily. Credit for the victory over the gods of Egypt was given to the Apollo of the island of Leucas, later revered as the Apollo of Actium. The temple on the Palatine Hill, which Octavian had vowed to build after the battle of Naulochos, was now dedicated to him. On the site of Octavian's camp a town was founded in honor of the victory and called Nicopolis. A monument testified to Octavian's gratitude to Neptune, Mars, and Apollo Actiacus, and every four years games were held to commemorate the turning point brought about by the battle of Actium.

Since Antony and Cleopatra organized a last-ditch effort to defend themselves in Egypt, a brief sequel to the battle of Actium was necessary. On August 1 in 30 BC Octavian and his army defeated Antony for a second time near Alexandria. Antony fell on his sword, dying in Cleopatra's arms. When the victor tried to capture the queen alive, in order to display her in his triumphal procession at home, she evaded his grasp by letting a poisonous snake bite her. Her suicide impressed even the Roman poet Horace, who wrote a poem expressing his respect (*Odes*, 1, 37). Although he had lost his prize trophy, Octavian had sufficient consolation. He, his forces, and his party had emerged from the conflict as the sole victors, and the empire was their reward. Furthermore he had won a rich new province for himself and for Rome. The wealth of the Egyptian royal family, which Octavian was able to seize after Cleopatra's suicide, along with revenues Egypt was forced to pay as a new Roman province and other war booty, allowed him to distribute lavish rewards to his supporters on an unprecedented scale. Rome had never seen anything like the three-day celebration of Octavian's threefold triumph – for his victories in Illyricum, Actium, and Alexandria – held in August of 29 BC. The festivities also marked the end of the two decades of civil war that had begun when Julius Caesar crossed the Rubicon. The atrocities, suffering, and uncertainty brought by war had left the population exhausted, and many of the families that had once dominated politics had been completely extirpated. In their place new men had risen to power, for whom the traditions of the republic were no longer living experience, but merely hollow shells.

What everyone shared was a desire for peace, and many were prepared to pay a high price for it. When Octavian ordered the Temple of Janus Quirinus in Rome to be closed in 29 BC, to mark the return of peace to the entire Roman state, he intended it to symbolize the start of a new era. Only two questions remained to be clarified: What form the government would take, now that the civil wars were over, and what position the victor would occupy in it.

7
A New Political Order: The Principate Takes Shape

The third-century Greek historian Cassius Dio, who was himself a member of the Senate, included in his *Roman History* a debate supposedly delivered before Octavian in the year 29 BC. The two speakers were Agrippa, who had actually won the battles that made Octavian sole ruler in Rome, and Maecenas, a shrewd, highly educated politician and a member of the old Etruscan nobility. Although Maecenas did not belong to the Senate and never served as a magistrate, preferring to stay in the background, Octavian had entrusted him with important and difficult missions. During the years 31–29 BC, when the victor of Actium was occupied in the East, Maecenas had looked after his interests in Rome and Italy.

Now, according to Cassius Dio, the two speakers offered their opinions about how the government in Rome ought to be organized following the end of the civil wars. Agrippa argued for a return to the republic, a step that would have required Octavian to relinquish the power he had won. Maecenas, on the other hand, not only favored creating an open and undisguised form of monarchy, but also offered detailed proposals for reorganizing the Senate, political offices, army, taxes, and the legal system. All in all, Maecenas' proposals amounted to sweeping reforms in the structure of government and many areas of life beyond it.

Of course the speeches reported by the historian were never delivered in this form; no one could have possibly anticipated such far-reaching changes or have developed a theoretical framework for them so early. Yet Cassius Dio's imagined debate reflects one aspect of the situation quite accurately: In the years following Actium, Octavian and his most trusted associates certainly discussed at length how to create a form of government that would leave power in their hands, but do so legally. We do not possess any specific details of these discussions, for they were not conducted in public. The days when such vital questions were debated openly in the Senate or the assembly of the Roman people were over. After Augustus came to power, bills were pre-arranged as a rule, and presented for formal passage only. As a result we can only speculate about the reasoning behind the decisions Octavian and his associates reached concerning a form of permanent rule.

Nonetheless two cornerstones of their reasoning are clear. First of all, Octavian had no intention of giving up the power he had acquired. Therefore a form of government had to be found that would preserve his position of power at its core. This was also in the interests of the Caesarian party. Octavian had not won his victory alone, and the participants in the struggle now expected a share of the rewards. Secondly, the model that Julius Caesar had been in the process of developing, namely a straightforward monarchy from which virtually all traces of the republican past had been eliminated, was politically unviable. That model had resulted in Julius Caesar's murder. After the traumatic events of the preceding decades, it was true, Roman citizens – especially the political elite – were far more inclined to accept rule by one man. But few would have favored an open overthrow of the old system.

The fundamental decision reached by Octavian and his political friends and advisers was therefore to restore the old republic, at least in name. It was what he had repeatedly declared to be his intention in the preceding years. However, during the last years of the republic legal instruments had been created to deal with emergencies and to accommodate the ambitions of men like Pompeius Magnus (Pompey the Great), Julius Caesar, and Crassus. (Although the constitution consisted to a large extent of tradition, new elements were always being added.) These measures had stretched the limits of what was "constitutional," i.e., politically feasible, and since they had been accepted some years before by the Senate and the people, it could be claimed that they already formed a part of Roman tradition. They now offered legal precedents that could be used to secure Octavian's power. Tactically it was mainly a question of choosing the right moment, so that the restoration of the republic and the confirmation of Octavian's power would appear both natural and complementary.

The leaders devoted the period after Antony's defeat to creating the right moment. Octavian was celebrated as the bringer of peace, and received honors intended to demonstrate the magnitude of his achievements. The priests of the state cult were instructed to include his name in all prayers and vows, particularly in the hymn of the Salians, a priesthood said to have been founded by Romulus. Both Octavian's birthday and the date of his victory at Actium were declared holidays. Citizens were told to offer sacrifices to his genius during their household devotions. And after a long interruption, the ceremony of the *augurium salutis* (augury for the prosperity of the state) was celebrated again, at which prayers to increase the well-being of the Roman people were offered to the gods, represented in this world by Octavian. All these measures, elevating him to a sphere above ordinary humanity, demonstrated that the very existence of the Roman polity was linked to his person, and probably owed their passage at this time to a combination of genuine convictions and political calculation.

Those so inclined could view these and further changes that were still to come against the backdrop of the preceding chaos. In Rome temples and shrines were restored. All Roman citizens were counted again in the first census for 40 years. The resulting tally of 4,063,000 citizens represented a fourfold increase since the last census in 69 BC and demonstrated Rome's strength. Augustus made a point of including the figure in the *Res Gestae*. In the year 30 BC Octavian also received the right to raise new men to the ranks of the patriciate. This was necessary because so many patrician families had been annihilated during the civil wars, yet such families performed essential functions in the community. Only patricians could serve as certain kinds of priests, but it was these priests' sacrifices that ensured the favor of the gods and thus the welfare of the whole nation. Octavian made use of his privilege the following year, creating a list of new patricians in which his political supporters figured prominently. And finally, in 28 BC, he declared invalid all the emergency measures that had been proclaimed during the civil wars in violation of existing law. Taking this step did not in fact limit his power significantly, although the declaration concerned his own past actions in large part. Presumably it created some freedom of action for him, by releasing him from earlier promises and agreements.

This was one of the decisive steps in restoring the republic, which – as Augustus himself pointed out in chapter 34 of the *Res Gestae* – took place during his sixth and seventh terms as consul (28 and 27 BC). It was an extended process, not the single act that Cassius Dio, our main source, suggests took place in early 27 BC. A recently published gold coin dating from Octavian's sixth consulate a year earlier, in 28 BC, commemorates the fact that he returned *iura et leges*, law and statutes, to the Roman people in that year. This probably meant first and foremost that free elections could take place, in name at least, and that law courts could operate without overt political pressure. Such reforms altered the political atmosphere, although we cannot be sure about how they were implemented in detail over the course of the year.

The final decisive act followed in January of 27 BC, although it was probably neither as dramatic nor as condensed as in Cassius Dio's account. The historian presents the return of power to the Senate as if it had been compressed into the space of a few days that January. While this is unlikely, Octavian's action was radical enough, for he relinquished his full and unlimited authority over the provinces and command of the legions stationed there, which were the real foundation of his power.

What Octavian's actual words to the Senate were, we do not know. But it is evident that both the summary provided by Cassius Dio and the implications of Octavian's own account in the *Res Gestae* represent half-truths. Octavian did indeed formally return the government to the Senate and the people of Rome, who were legally sovereign. In theory they once again became the final authority for important decisions. In reality, however, they had very little authority to decide anything, as they lacked the power to initiate legislation – to introduce any bills for debate. More importantly, however, Octavian's relinquishment of his provinces and their army did not reduce him to the status of an ordinary citizen. He remained consul, for he did not resign the consulship he shared with Marcus Agrippa in 27 BC, and thus continued to possess the foremost power of initiative in the state. In addition he possessed the loyalty not only of the soldiers currently serving in the legions, but also of the veterans. He had countless clients and adherents – people who depended on his patronage – in every part of the realm, and his financial resources were unrivaled. This translated into power at all levels of politics and society, as all senators were well aware. Above all, however, most of them realized that Octavian had not the slightest intention of really surrendering power. Some of them had especially good cause to know, because they had been coached in the roles they were to play after his announcement.

When the Senate began to discuss Octavian's speech, their moment had come. It was obvious how much all Roman citizens owed to the son of Caesar, they responded. The peace that had finally returned was his achievement, and his name, as guarantor of the common welfare, had been included in public prayers for good reason. The gods were obliged to protect him for the sake of Rome. How could Octavian think of deserting the Roman people and allowing chaos to return? The frontier provinces were not yet completely pacified, and Rome's relationship with the Parthians remained precarious. They pleaded with him not to withdraw in a time of great need. The state needed him, preferably with all the powers he had exercised so successfully in the preceding years.

Octavian refused, as he obviously had to. If he had acceded to the senators' request, the entire effect of returning power to the Senate and people, in the process he had begun in the year 28, would have been lost. But then bit by bit he gave in to the senators' pressure to take charge again, and finally he agreed to assume responsibility for the provinces where peace was not fully established. It turned out to be a considerable portion of the empire, despite the earlier closing of the Temple of Janus: all of Spain and Gaul, Syria, Cilicia, Cyprus, and – of course – Egypt. It was no accident that the territory included Spain, Gaul, and Syria, the regions assigned to the triumvirs Julius Caesar, Pompey, and Crassus in 55 BC. Now these three provinces and more were to be placed under a single command. It became apparent that this was a step in the direction of rule over the entire empire by one man. Nevertheless, the power that now became concentrated in Octavian's hands in such an irreproachably legal manner was not intended to resemble a monarchy, or even kingship for life. Therefore Octavian accepted command of the provinces for a limited time only – a period of ten years. That amount of time was sufficient to subdue them; he promised that if he succeeded in pacifying any of them before the ten years were up, he would return responsibility for them to the Senate.

The rationale behind this decision took the provinces themselves into account, but even more important were the legions stationed in them; while they did not constitute the whole Roman army, they did represent the bulk of it. Further legions were based in Illyricum, Macedonia, Pamphylia, and Africa, provinces that were not assigned to Octavian but were known instead as "provinces of the Roman people." Nevertheless the majority of legions were once again under Octavian's command – and this had been his key aim all along. It was not necessary for the Senate to appoint him to a further office or delegate further powers to him for Octavian to carry out his duties; he was already consul, and as such his legitimate powers – his *imperium* – permitted him to govern provinces and command the troops stationed in them, as in the republican era. Octavian had found a very simple and effective way to legalize his power, and secure it. The outward form was not new; Pompey had already governed the Spanish provinces as consul in 55 BC, without ever leaving Rome. He had dispatched senators as his representatives, or legates, to carry out his instructions and oversee specific tasks. This was exactly the concept adopted by Octavian. The governors of the other provinces, the Roman people's provinces, were chosen by lot from among the members of the Senate.

Compared with the obvious preeminence that Octavian had possessed before, the new distribution of power looked on the surface like a weakening of his position. In fact, however, he had gained far more than he had lost. Now his position no longer rested on a vague "universal consensus" proclaimed during a time of chaos, but on official Senate decrees and a proper consulship. And he could claim – correctly – that the Senate had pleaded with him to take on his extra duties. When Augustus stresses in chapter 34 of the *Res Gestae* that since that time he has surpassed all others in influence (*auctoritas*) while never possessing more power by virtue of his office than his fellow magistrates, the statement is accurate. What he glosses over is the very firm foundation on which that influence rested: his command over several provinces and the legions stationed there, his incomparable financial resources, and a vast network of clients. In Rome he had his own body guards, the Praetorian Guard, at his disposal, and since their loyalty was crucial to his remaining alive, the first motion passed by the senators after Octavian returned command of the provinces and army to them was an order to double the guards' pay. The term *auctoritas* by itself sounds harmless enough, but one must not lose sight of what really counted, namely the sources of concrete power behind it. Nevertheless it served extremely well as ideological camouflage for concealing Octavian's actual position as sole ruler. In fact Octavian occupied a unique position even officially, despite his claims to the contrary, for he was consul. That office permitted him to dictate policy to the Senate and assembly of the plebs in Rome, while at the same time he controlled large regions of the provincial empire. No other office-holder could even begin to compare with him.

The Senate celebrated the new legal and political configuration of the years 28 and 27 BC as the "restoration of the republic." The phrase applied to the real situation only when viewed against the background of decades of civil war and the legally sanctioned dictatorship of the triumvirate. A true restoration of the old political system, in which a free Senate governed and the leading noble families competed to advance their own interests in the assembly of the people, was no longer possible. But an appearance of a return to the old ways was achieved, accompanied by a glimmer of liberty.

The Senate and People felt obliged to invent new and unique honors to express their gratitude to the man responsible for these illusory gains. They hit upon the idea of mounting a golden shield in the Senate chamber that listed his four cardinal virtues: valor, clemency, justice, and piety. The senators declared that one could cite countless examples of Octavian's outstanding qualities, which he embodied in ideal fashion. Not only had he avenged the murder of Julius Caesar, for example; he had also pardoned many of his opponents after the battle of Actium, freely and without compulsion. Nonetheless some citizens remained skeptical about such an idealized portrait, particularly when Octavian was awarded the civic crown, depicting a laurel wreath, bestowed on those who had saved Roman citizens from death. Coins depicting the crown bore the motto *ob cives servatos*, "for the rescue of citizens." Not everyone had forgotten past actions such as Octavian's orders to slaughter the citizens of Perusia after he had taken the city.

In the long run, however, the most important honor he received was the Senate's conferral of a new appellation for the ruler: the name *Augustus*, sometimes translated as "the illustrious one." On this occasion, too, the Senate's action was far from spontaneous; Octavian's associates had deliberated at length about a possible cognomen that would distinguish him from all other Romans. For a time Octavian himself had favored *Romulus*, as a way of comparing his accomplishments to a second founding of Rome. But the name was too closely associated with the notion of kingship, and Octavian and his party wished to avoid references to monarchy at all costs. Furthermore there was a legend in circulation according to which Romulus had been murdered – literally torn to pieces – by senators enraged at his tyranny. Under those circumstances the name might have been a bad omen, reminding people too much of Julius Caesar and his fate. As a result the new and more innocuous name *Augustus* was chosen which, if it had any associations at all, linked the bearer with the sphere of religion. It was Munatius Plancus, the turncoat of the year 32, who introduced the motion in the Senate; we can be sure he was following instructions.

From then on the son of Julius Caesar bore a unique name; no other Roman could make the same claim. By the start of the thirties, or even earlier, he had also begun calling himself *Imperator Caesar divi filius*, "Imperator Caesar son of the deified one." This represented an extraordinary innovation, since not one of the name's elements corresponded to tradition. The use of *Imperator* as a name suggested a permanent link with the Roman tradition of victory. Until then a family named "Caesar" had never existed; it was merely the cognomen of one branch of the Julian family. By turning Caesar into a family name, Augustus introduced a new family – namely one that began with himself – into the annals of Rome. And finally, only Augustus could boast a father who had been declared immortal. When the Senate added the cognomen *Augustus*, probably on January 16, 27 BC, it created what appeared to be an ordinary three-part Roman name, *Imp. Caesar Augustus*, yet at the same time it was unprecedented.

None of the parts represented a title or reflected his official position. As long as Augustus lived, it was merely a name. Only after his successors adopted these components and added them to their own names did they gradually acquire the function of a title. Any one of the three components could then signify the supreme ruler in Rome, and two of them continued in use in later centuries in various European languages to denote the highest conceivable political authority: *emperor, Kaiser, czar.* Strictly speaking, however, Augustus was *not* an emperor, neither after the introduction of the new political order in 28–27 BC nor later. This is a point to which we shall return. Officially he occupied the position of the first or chief man in the state, the *princeps*, to whom the Senate and people had delegated responsibility for the welfare of the citizens. During the republican period several such *principes* had always con- ducted the affairs of the commonwealth; now there was only one. Tasks were entrusted to him as an individual, and he exer- cised his influence (*auctoritas*) for the benefit of all. In this manner he could be said to have earned his position as first in the state. The new form of rule created by these arrangements was the principate. It was by no means created in one stroke in the year 27, however. Its full development took place over many years, with the system not reaching its final form until around the time of Augustus' death. It was precisely such slow development, a process advancing without abrupt adjustments for the most part, that ensured general acceptance of the principate in the population. One of Augustus' favorite maxims ran *festina lente!*, roughly "slow and steady wins the race." He had learned that one usually could accomplish more that way than with impetuous haste.

8
The Principate Develops Further

As we have seen, a general framework for the new order was created in 28–27 BC, but many details remained unresolved. Individual citizens lacked guidelines and experience in how to act; they had no way of knowing where the bounds of acceptable political behavior lay. And so they had no choice but to discover the new rules through a process of trial and error in their dealings with one another and with their ruler. In the first few years of the new regime, some Romans paid for their failure to sense the location of the invisible limits with their careers, while others paid with their lives. Those who learned quickly just where the perils lurked provided useful examples for their fellow citizens.

One man named C. Cornelius Gallus offered a prime example of what not to do. After the final defeat of Antony and Cleopatra, Octavian chose Gallus as his representative in Egypt and placed him in charge there as prefect, or governor. Control of a rich province where three legions were based was a position of great trust, and Gallus was exceptionally fortunate to be granted it, as he was not a member of the Senate, previously a requirement for a provincial governorship. However, Gallus failed to grasp the degree of restraint with which Octavian expected him to manage affairs in Egypt, and began to regard himself as successor to the pharaohs and the dynasty of the Ptolemies. Perhaps he did not give orders for statues of himself to be erected everywhere, with inscriptions praising his own deeds instead of those of his superior in Rome. But at the very least he tolerated such monuments. Inscriptions honoring Gallus were also carved on the pyramids, those conspicuous symbols of royal power and status, and even on the sacred island of Philae in the Nile, so we can imagine the kind of propaganda campaign for himself that Gallus probably initiated. When reports of these occurrences reached Rome, they were regarded as scandalous breaches of political loyalty. Augustus withdrew his favor and friendship, and that spelled the end of Gallus' career. After ordering an investigation, the Senate confiscated his property. Gallus took the only way out and committed suicide.

Gallus' case disturbed Augustus deeply, for the prefect had been one of his closest associates. If such a trusted supporter failed to recognize the limits of appropriate behavior in the new political order, what could he expect from his opponents? When Licinius Crassus, a grandson of Julius Caesar's ally of the same name, returned from a campaign in Macedonia, he expressed a desire to exceed the bounds of the usual triumph by personally dedicating to Jupiter the armor of the enemy general he had slain. Such a ceremony would have represented a public celebration of the highest order of valor, suggesting that Crassus surpassed even Augustus himself in this virtue. The princeps could not or would not permit it, so legal technicalities were cited to prevent the dedication. Crassus' display of excessive ambition put an abrupt end to his political career, too.

Augustus probably sensed that Romans would need time to grow accustomed to the new order, but he did not want to be perceived to be manipulating the process too obviously. This may be one reason why he left the capital in mid-27 on a trip to Gaul. Early in the year 26 he moved on to northern Spain, where two tribes, the Asturians and Cantabrians, were mounting strong resistance to Roman domination. Mainly, however, his journey was intended to demonstrate how seriously he took the responsibility that had been delegated to him for both provinces – namely to subdue areas in which lasting peace had still to be established. As an added benefit, Augustus' sojourn outside Italy strengthened his ties with both current soldiers and veterans, a good number of whom had been settled in southern France and parts of Spain including Emerita (present-day Merida).

During Augustus' absence Romans of all political persuasions, even those who had held themselves aloof from politics, must have discussed the current situation and the future. What should they make of their "restored liberty," and how much latitude did they really have? Augustus had declared that all the institutions and officers of the government should carry out their traditional functions, including the assembly of the people, the Senate, and the magistrates. But how far could they do so without risking a conflict with the princeps? He had occupied one of the two consulships without interruption since the year 31 BC, after all. That was hardly in keeping with republican tradition, which had dictated after a man had served as consul he could not be re-elected for ten years. Now, however, at least one consulship appeared to be permanent, a circumstance that cut in half the opportunities for both members of the old nobility and of Augustus' own party to hold that office themselves. Had they contributed so little to his victory, they must have asked themselves, that he could deny them advancement to the highest rank of both the magistracy and the Senate, as consuls and former consuls? In addition there were signs that some very young men might soon overtake them. In the year 25 BC Claudius Marcellus, son of Augustus' sister Octavia by her first husband, married Julia, the princeps' only daughter. When Marcellus was elected aedile the following year, at the age of only 18, he was simultaneously given the right to stand for consul ten years before reaching the minimum age prescribed by law. Both steps represented significant departures from tradition. What achievements could Marcellus point to, apart from the fact that he was Augustus' nephew and son-in-law? Such indications of special privilege could not help but dismay the princeps' own partisans as well as those who had remained politically uncommitted. Reports circulated that Marcellus had been designated as Augustus' successor, should the princeps die. During the trial of one Marcus Primus, a former proconsul of Macedonia, the accused claimed in his defense that he had committed the act for which he had been charged – conducting a military campaign outside the borders of Macedonia – on the instructions not only of Augustus, but also of Marcellus. That had to be regarded as a warning signal.

In the year 23 BC, feeling against Augustus must have led to a crisis, although today it is difficult to ascertain the details of what happened. It appears, however, that a conspiracy against him arose, in which his fellow consul, a certain Terentius Varro Murena, may have been involved. In any event Varro Murena did not serve out his full term. Unfortunately the precise reasons for his early departure from office are unknown, because a crucial part is missing from the marble slabs containing the official list of consuls, known as the *Fasti Capitolini*. In any event the conspiracy was uncovered during the trial of Marcus Primus. The participants in the conspiracy were identified, placed on trial themselves, and quickly sentenced to death; those who had managed to flee were tracked down and executed.

Varro Murena was replaced as consul by Calpurnius Piso, who had supported the republican cause after Julius Caesar was murdered but had maintained his distance from public life since. To have gained the participation of such a noted republican as his co-consul was certainly a victory for Augustus, and was meant to demonstrate that he was prepared to cooperate with all political parties. But at the same time it showed that he, too, had to make concessions.

It was a time of extreme stress for Augustus. Finding the right path in the elaborate and complex new system was not easy, and he was learning along with the others. It would not be surprising if the demands on him were the cause of the serious illness he developed in the late spring of 23 BC. Augustus was forced to consider who would carry on his legacy if he died. On his sickbed he handed over his signet ring to Agrippa, but he gave a list of the troops in his provinces and an account of public finances to his co-consul Piso. It was an ingeniously balanced move to demonstrate that both adherents from his party and the duly chosen officers of the state had a role to play. To the relief of many Romans, Augustus had not chosen a successor. Strictly speaking there had been no need to, and if he had named someone at that point, he could have destroyed most of the system he had begun to put in place. The proper political instruments for such a step had not yet been developed.

What the consequences would have been of dividing political responsibility as Augustus had indicated remained unknown, for the princeps recovered. He drew his own conclusions from his illness, however, with consequences for both his own supporters and other leading senators. He gave up his permanent consulship and stood for election only twice more after a very long interval, in order to introduce his two adopted sons, Gaius and Lucius, to their public roles as adult citizens in the years 5 and 2 BC.

By giving up the consulship Augustus ceased to be directly in charge of the political scene in Rome itself, but his position with respect to the provinces remained unchanged. He retained the functions he had carried out as consul, but now as a proconsul. (This emerges clearly from an edict for Hispania Citerior issued by Augustus himself in 15 BC, in which *proconsul* is listed among his titles.) However, his proconsular authority extended only to provinces specifically delegated to him, and not to the provinces of the Roman people, which had their own proconsuls, chosen by lot from among the senators. As consul, Augustus had clearly been able to intervene in their sphere as well, if he considered it necessary to restore order, as an inscription from Cyme in the province of Asia shows. Truly losing the power to intervene legally in the political affairs of all provinces would have been a significant restriction, however, so once again a solution had to be found. This time it was a precedent from the time of Pompey that had already proved useful to Brutus and Cassius in the year 43 BC. Augustus' *imperium* was granted a special status. (It is still a matter of debate whether his *imperium* was defined as superior to that of other proconsuls – an *imperium maius* – as certainly occurred later under his successor Tiberius.) In any event, if a disagreement arose between Augustus and another proconsul, the regulation allowed him to intercede as he saw fit. Furthermore it was decreed that his powers of office did not expire if he crossed the sacred city limits of Rome. According to republican law the appointment of a proconsul ended automatically at the moment he returned from his province and crossed the *pomerium*. Augustus received his exemption from this rule without a specified time limit, but it was understood to depend on his continuing as proconsul. Once again he was placed on a plane above the normal order.

In Rome itself, Augustus' appointment as proconsul with a provincial *imperium* limited his political options. In particular his office did not enable him to convene the Senate or the assembly of the people, the only two bodies that could formally enact laws. But once again Augustus and his advisers came up with a substitute. The Senate conferred on him the full powers of a tribune of the people (*tribunicia potestas*), although not the office itself. In addition a separate resolution gave Augustus the power to bypass the normal procedures and convene the Senate at any time. In this manner a whole range of powers and privileges were created for him, to give a legal foundation to his political role. The tribunician power, which implied an obligation to protect the rights of the people, became the emblem of the new regime. It was counted in years, so that the total number of years he held the power resembled the length of a reign. Augustus included it among his official titles, in contrast to proconsul, which was not normally listed and occurs only in the edict of El Bierzo in Spain. But perhaps his new praenomen, *Imp(erator)*, functioned as a substitute for the *imperium* of a proconsul.

For all those Romans who continued to look to the republican past as a standard, the new arrangement was not very satisfactory, but it deprived them of the obvious and compelling objection to the system, namely that Augustus was blocking access to the consulship by occupying it permanently himself. Members of Augustus' party could also be pleased about the prominence now given to one of their number, Agrippa, as the ruler's second-in-command. Like Augustus, Agrippa received an *imperium* like that of a proconsul in the year 23 BC. It was limited to the East and to a term of five years, however, so that it ended before Augustus' ten-year *imperium*. These circumstances clearly reflected the existing hierarchy in the distribution of power. The princeps made a concession to the senators in the republican camp by choosing from their ranks both his successor as consul in the year 23 and the two consuls of 22, a step that helped to pacify the republicans and integrate them into his government. The plebs in the city of Rome were discontented, however, because they felt their interests were no longer being looked after sufficiently.

When food shortages occurred in 22 BC, the plebs wanted to force Augustus to become dictator; cynics accused him of having engineered the situation on purpose. In a theatrical gesture of refusal he tore his clothing and bared his breast, saying he would rather be stabbed to death by the mob's daggers than reintroduce the dictatorship, which Antony had abolished by law in 44 BC. But Augustus did agree to take over direct responsibility for food supplies in the city (the *cura annonae*), as Pompey had done previously. The danger of famine receded within a short time. Augustus also refused to become censor, the officer in charge of carrying out the census and revising the rolls of the Senate and the *equites*. However, the two men selected as censors in his place failed to carry out their duties. Romans took that as a sign that only Augustus could now perform this kind of public function successfully. The more often similar failures occurred, the more people tended to accept the princeps' unique position in the state.

Within the next few years a disturbance at the time of consular elections seemed to show once more that the old ways would not work without his participation. Augustus, who had traveled to Sicily and then to the East, refused to become consul himself. But in his absence no one could overcome the chaotic situation in the capital, not even Agrippa, whom Augustus dispatched from the East to take charge. The princeps himself stayed behind, as negotiations on an important treaty with the Parthians were underway, and he was unwilling to endanger them. He did not return until the autumn of 19 BC. As he approached Rome, a group of leading senators, praetors, and tribunes of the people came out to meet him – a unique honor, as Augustus later stressed in the *Res Gestae*. He also mentioned a further honor. At this time the Senate also ordered that an altar to Fortuna Redux, the goddess who had watched over his return, be set up on the Appian Way near the Porta Capena. The day of his return was declared a holiday, to be celebrated annually with sacrifices and games, known as the Augustalia. All of this indicates how precarious the situation in Rome had become, and how necessary Augustus' intervention appeared to many people. Such formal displays of gratitude did not occur in the conditions of the early principate without good reason.

The specific legal and political consequences of this crisis remain a matter of debate among scholars. It is certain, however, that in 19 BC. Augustus received new rights associated with the consulate and the scope that office offered for political action. He mentions in the *Res Gestae* that he twice conducted a census with the power of a consul (*consulari cum imperio*), in the years 8 BC and 14 AD, although it was not expressly conferred on him for these occasions. This means that he must have already possessed it. But since on the other hand it is impossible for one man to have possessed the supreme legal authority, an *imperium*, twice, the *imperium consulare* must have been identical with his *imperium* as proconsul. If that is so, we are then forced to conclude that Augustus did not receive a further *imperium* in the year 19; rather his *imperium* as proconsul, which up to that time had been valid only in the provinces, was now extended to Rome and Italy. In theory this new right was not expressly limited to a particular period, just as no limitations had been placed on Augustus' right to cross the *pomerium*. But since the right depended on Augustus' commission in the provinces, it was in fact subject to that commission's time limits. With the extension of his *imperium* Augustus also acquired the right to use the symbols of the highest magistracy in the republican system, the consul's chair (*sella curulis*) and the twelve servants called lictors with the symbolic bundles of rods (*fasces*) also in the city of Rome. Thus in terms of his legal possibilities for taking action, Augustus was placed an equal footing with the consuls. In any event, no further disturbances at elections, which were supervised by the consuls as a rule, are reported from the following period.

With these new powers, Augustus' development of his political position had essentially reached its final form; later *principes* based their powers chiefly on the same array of legal competencies. However, the period of political reorientation was not yet concluded. The question of the army and of senators' access to military command remained to be settled.

Perhaps it was no accident that the last triumph celebrated in Rome by a proconsul with an *imperium* independent from Augustus took place in that same year 19 BC. The victor was Cornelius Balbus, governor of Africa, who had defeated the Garamantes there. Balbus' family came from Gades (present-day Cadiz in Spain); he was the first man of provincial origin to be permitted a triumph – and the last ever. His name ends the register of commanders to be granted such a procession, which was inscribed on a triumphal arch for Augustus in the Forum Romanum.

Cornelius Balbus' victory was not the last successful campaign for Roman generals by any means, but later victors were not granted a triumphal procession. One reason for this was the fact that large forces tended to be commanded by legates, i.e. deputies of the princeps in the provinces. Any victories they achieved were credited to Augustus, under whose command they had officially served. Another reason was that peace tended to prevail in provinces governed by proconsuls with an independent *imperium*, which were less threatened by external and internal enemies, with the possible exception of Illyricum. And this province was finally assigned to Augustus in 11 BC; from then on it was governed by one of his legates instead of a proconsul. Yet even the proconsuls of Africa, who then became the sole remaining provincial governors in charge of a legion, stood under Augustus' command, at least at times. When Cornelius Lentulus, proconsul of Africa around 6 AD, won a victory over the Gaetulian tribe, he acted as Augustus' subordinate, and merely led the campaign like one of the princeps' legates.

A more important indicator in the general reorientation process was provided by Agrippa, who had his own *imperium* independent from Augustus from 23 on, but refused several times to accept the triumphal processions offered to him by the Senate after military victories. Instead he allowed Augustus to book the successes, with the result that by 13 AD

Augustus had been acclaimed as *imperator* for important victories a total of 21 times. If a man like Agrippa, who came closest to matching the princeps in power and prestige, hung back and let Augustus appear as the sole source of Roman military success, how could anyone else claim the right to a victory celebration? Even Tiberius and Drusus, Augustus' stepsons, were not permitted to enter Rome in triumph after military victories in Germany and Illyricum, although the Senate had voted to offer this honor to both of them. Only after more than a decade had passed, when it had become clear to everyone that both command of the army and the concept of victory belonged to the princeps, did Augustus allow members of his own family to celebrate triumphs – and them alone. Rome did not experience a full-scale triumphal procession again until 12 years after that of Cornelius Balbus, when Tiberius celebrated the victory he had achieved in Germany, the sphere of his *imperium* as proconsul. All the others who fought successful battles in the name of the princeps had to be content with insignia, the *ornamenta triumphalia*, as a surrogate. In time the commanders became accustomed to such decorations, and even proud to receive them. A bronze statue of a man honored in this fashion was also placed on the new Forum of Augustus, giving visible form to the correct hierarchy – and the new order.

Reality in these years embraced the paradox of traditional Republican forms and simultaneous emphasis on the princeps' special position. In the year 18 BC Augustus' ten-year *imperium* for his provinces ended; it was extended for the period of five years only. We do not know the reasoning behind this decision, but presumably the argument was advanced that the state could not exist without his leadership. At that time Agrippa's *imperium* was also renewed, and he also received the powers of a tribune, like Augustus, from the year 18 on. In the same year Agrippa and Augustus carried out the difficult and risky task of revising the roll of Senate members. There were two men who shared the burden of concern for Rome and its power, but only one of them was princeps. When, in 17 BC, Augustus' daughter Julia and her husband Agrippa had a second son named Lucius, Augustus adopted both him and his older brother, Gaius, who had been born in the year 20 BC. Everyone understood the meaning of his gesture, without his having to spell the message out directly: "I see the future in them, my 'successors' whom I cannot officially name as such." At the time no one could anticipate how differently things would turn out. For the moment, the princeps' intentions were what counted. The future of Augustus' family, the *domus Augusta*, was closely linked to the future of the Roman people.

Shortly before adopting the boys, Augustus had provided another important sign by announcing that it was time to celebrate the Secular Games (*ludi saeculares*). According to old Etruscan tradition the life of a people or nation was cyclical: When no one remained alive who had witnessed the beginning of a new century (*saeculum*), a new one began. Now Etruscan seers declared that the condition had been met, and in addition a comet appeared that was interpreted as a return of the *sidus Iulium* announcing the start of a new century or age. As head of the priestly college of the "fifteen men," Augustus was in charge of the festival together with Agrippa; it ran from the end of May to mid-June and included sacrifices, circus games, baiting of bears or other animals, and theater performances. The entire populace was expected to participate – even women in mourning for a family member, who were usually excluded – to symbolize the renewal of the whole community. The deities celebrated at the festival were Apollo, the special patron of the princeps, and Apollo's sister, the goddess Diana. Horace addressed them in the lines of the hymn he wrote for the occasion (the *carmen saeculare*), asking their protection for the Roman people and the ruler on the Palatine Hill, Augustus. So that later generations would not forget the beginning of this new age in Rome, an account of the Secular Games was inscribed on two pillars, one of bronze and one of marble. Large sections of the marble pillar can be viewed today in Rome's Termi Museum.

Some contemporaries must have regarded the start of the new *saeculum* in a spirit of resignation, for the process of identifying Rome with Augustus was already well advanced. That efforts were once again made to increase links with past traditions did not alter this fact. The families of the old nobility provided almost all the consuls from the end of the 20s on, and another old custom was revived by having the senators acting as masters of the mint issue new coins. Of course they were less and less able to adorn them with images of themselves and their own families, as had been possible in the old days of the republic; Augustus and his achievements took up more and more of the space on them. Political opposition to the princeps existed, but the senators unwilling to cooperate with him, a rather small number in any case, tended to withdraw from public life rather than stay on and express their opposition. What meaning could their own role in politics have, after all, when the majority of the Senate and the people designated the princeps' two adopted sons as future consuls at the age of 14? Five years later they were to carry the *fasces*. A blood relationship with the ruler replaced merit and achievements as a qualification for office, as in the earlier case of Claudius Marcellus, and some naturally felt a sense of frustration.

For the great majority of Romans of all ranks including the senatorial class, however, the memory of republican ideals faded increasingly under the demands of practical day-to-day life. People adapted to existing conditions, accepting that they would have to look out for their own interests as best they could. This only helped Augustus, for even when unexpected events threatened his plans – Agrippa died suddenly in 12 BC, followed by both of Augustus' adopted sons, Lucius in AD 2 and Gaius in AD 4 – his power as such was never seriously in danger. In legal terms this position remained unaltered after 19 BC, except for his election as high priest (*pontifex maximus*); he added this title to his collection after Lepidus, the former triumvir who had long outlived his era in power, finally died in 12 BC. People streamed into Rome to vote on March 6; Augustus reported in chapter 10 of the *Res Gestae* that never before had so many Roman citizens assembled to participate in an election. In his new office he was officially recognized as Rome's highest-ranking representative in dealing with the gods. Augustus responded in a manner that we can now recognize as typical for him – namely by reviving another republican tradition. He renewed the priesthood for Jupiter the Best and Greatest (*Iupiter Optimus Maximus*) and appointed a priest, known as the *flamen Dialis*, for the first time since the holder of that office had been murdered in 87 BC. In addition, Augustus as high priest was now responsible for the Vestal Virgins and able to appoint new members to their order. Because the Vestals guarded the sacred flame that guaranteed the continued existence of the *res publica*, they, like Augustus himself, served as protectors of Rome. The princeps decided to combine these two spheres symbolically by making part of his house on the Palatine Hill the official residence of the *pontifex maximus* and making it over to the public, as tradition demanded. There he also created a shrine to Vesta and placed his wife, Livia, in charge of guarding its sacred flame. Such repeated symbolic acts added new dimensions to his public position, increasing his identification with Rome in the eyes of the masses.

The crowning act in this series was Augustus' acclamation as *pater patriae*, the father of his country. His decision to end the *Res Gestae* with it reveals how important this honor was to him. The Senate, equestrian order, and people had pressed him to accept the title, and finally he agreed. On February 5 in the year 2 BC, Marcus Valerius Messalla Corvinus, who had been Octavian's co-consul in the fateful year 31, presented the resolution in the Senate with the concurrence of the other social orders. This universal recognition was recorded in inscriptions in the entrance hall of Augustus' house on the Palatine Hill, in the chamber of the Senate on the Forum Romanum, and under the quadriga (a chariot with four horses) in front of the Temple of Mars in Augustus' own forum, and also in his full list of titles, which had arrived at its final form with the addition of *pater patriae*. The designation must have given him immense satisfaction, because it reflected the notion that through his far-sighted planning (*providentia*) he had ensured Rome's welfare for the future, as a father would do for his family. His two adopted sons, although young, had already served in public office and would be able to carry on in his place. So Augustus must have hoped, but the reality would be quite different (see chapter 14).

9
The Princeps and the Roman Elite

In the *Res Gestae* the Senate plays a very prominent role. Augustus mentions it almost immediately, in connection with the decrees it passed to admit him to membership as a young man. Many years later, while serving as consul in the year AD 100, the senator Pliny the Younger referred to the emperor Trajan as "one of us." The members of the Senate could have said the same of Octavian in the year 43 BC, although many of them would have had reservations about granting him their elevated status. The young man had not yet won their trust, nor had he achieved any distinction. In fact he had not even achieved the minimum age for joining the Senate. In 2 BC, when the senators awarded the title *pater patriae* to Augustus, they could also have called him "one of us," since officially he retained his membership. By that time, however, the situation had reversed itself; a number of senators would have hesitated to place the princeps on the same level as themselves, since he so far outranked them in power and prestige. Yet Augustus himself might have accepted the statement, for it reflected a fundamental premise of Roman political thinking: Anyone who played a role in the country's political life, or aspired to such a role, either belonged to the Senate or hoped to join it, for membership in that body was the sole path to political legitimacy. The coming of the new political order did not alter this basic principle. Octavian's rise to power took place in a process of dispute and reaching consensus with the Senate, and this applies even more to his later rule as princeps. Furthermore, since almost all his political allies and opponents belonged to the Senate, any biography of Augustus must also be a history of the Senate and its members in those same decades.

When Octavian gave up his emergency powers in 28–27 BC, the Senate's legal authority was restored in its former scope. Politically, however, the world had changed. Augustus was consul – *merely* consul, one might say – and as such he had no powers beyond what consuls had traditionally possessed. On the other hand he was in charge of most of the large provinces and commanded the legions stationed in them; this gave him an obvious position of dominance that could not help but affect the legislators' daily deliberations, as all of them were aware. Another factor that contributed even more to his dominance was the new composition of the Senate. Many of the old senatorial families had died out during the civil wars; others had become so impoverished that they could survive only with support from Augustus. Those who became financially dependent on him ceased to have an independent voice and influence in politics. Even more importantly, Julius Caesar had altered the Senate by making his chief supporters members, a trend increased by the triumvirs and finally by Augustus himself. These new men came from a different political background than the old families. The majority came from regions of Italy that had not been represented in the republic, and some belonged to tribes that had attained full Roman citizenship only two generations earlier, during the Social War. Such senators were from ethnic groups such as the Samnites or Peligni, or came from regions like Etruria or Umbria.

Leaders from areas north of the Apennines also first gained entry into Rome's political class at this time. They tended to

give their loyalty to the man who had made their full participation in Roman politics possible – originally Julius Caesar,
and later his political heir, Octavian. Claudius, the third
successor to Augustus, remarked long afterwards that the first
princeps had admitted to the Senate the elite from all colonies
and towns, who were naturally all respected and affluent men.
He was referring not only to the elite of Italy; in filling the
Senate roster Augustus drew on the reservoir of suitable men
available in several provinces, mainly southern Gaul and Spain,
where the inhabitants had adopted the Latin language and
Roman culture many generations earlier. Cornelius Balbus,
for example, the last senator permitted to celebrate a triumph
in Rome, came from Gades in Andalusia (see page 61).
Augustus' policy set in motion a process that ultimately transformed the Senate into a body where, by the end of the second
century AD, almost every part of the empire was represented.
By that time the ethnic groups subjected by the Romans were
participating in Roman rule on the same basis as the inhabitants of Italy – a development that no one could have anticipated in Augustus' own day.

The means available to Augustus to alter the makeup of the
Senate remained those of the republican era. The census was
one tool for removing members, and being elected as quaestor
was a way to join. Augustus did not have the power to create
new senators by appointing individuals directly to one of the
senatorial ranks, such as the class of former quaestors or praetors, at least not after the restoration of the traditional order.
Trying to reclaim that power would have been politically risky,
for it would have reminded citizens too much of Julius Caesar's
dictatorial style. Nevertheless, goals Augustus regarded as essential could be achieved using traditional methods; one of them
was to reduce the size of the Senate. After Actium its roster
had swollen to more than a thousand members, far in excess
of the six hundred that had become the rule in the time of
Sulla. The first pruning of the Senate rolls in 29–28 BC took

quite moderate form. Only obviously unworthy men were forced to leave – meaning those whose backgrounds deviated too markedly from the generally accepted norms. Some of Augustus' political opponents were also ejected at this time. However, their removal was not the main purpose of the cuts, and the ranks of the opposition from families with distinguished records, including men like Calpurnius Piso (see page 55f.), remained unscathed. The truly drastic cuts did not take place until 18 BC, when more than 300 senators lost their seats, most of them being compelled to resign. Augustus had attempted a policy of encouraging voluntary resignation at first, assuring senators that they would retain their honorary privileges if they complied, but very few took up his offer. Next he tried a complicated plan under which the senatorial class itself was to make the desired cuts. When that failed, Augustus took on the unwelcome task personally. Many of the men he forced out at this time appeared so dangerously resentful that Augustus appeared in the Senate wearing armor under his tunic. Yet by such radical means he succeeded in bringing the senate membership down to 600, where it remained until the late third century AD.

One of the criteria for measuring the "worthiness" of a senator was his net worth, and his corresponding income. A minimum level of wealth had been required before, but until Augustus' reform it had amounted to only 400,000 sesterces and had applied to knights and senators alike. The new rules demanded proof of assets amounting to at least a million sesterces for senators, and thus established a significant barrier between the senatorial and equestrian orders. The reform was intended to give the *ordo senatorius* a more distinct identity. One of its consequences, however, was to put an end to the traditional right of every Roman, so long as he was free-born and possessed the minimum required wealth, to run for public office, become a magistrate, and eventually reach the Senate. After the reform, only those men who were already entitled to wear a tunic with a broad purple stripe, the mark of senatorial rank, could present themselves as candidates. From the time of Augustus on, sons of senators acquired this status automatically, but others had to apply for it. It is possible that Augustus could award the right himself; if that is so, it offered him an elegant way to decide which new families could have access to Senate membership.

Above and beyond these general requirements, the way into the Senate remained election by the people. However in practice only a tiny percentage of Romans eligible to vote actually participated in the elections, mainly for practical reasons. Most of them lived much too far from Rome, but others did not bother to vote, realizing that the electorate had very little actual choice in any case. In the first few years after 27 BC some candidates waged hard-fought campaigns, and more such battles occurred after Augustus resigned his permanent consulship in 23 BC. But from 19 BC on, there is hardly any documentation of contested elections. This may be an accident related to the types of records that survived, but more likely it reflects the growing power of the princeps. He could influence elections through his power to accept or reject applications of aspiring candidates for various offices, but he could also announce his backing for individual candidates, for whom citizens were then obliged to vote. After a while some offices, particularly quaestor and tribune of the people, suffered from a noticeable lack of candidates; too many people had realized that there was little point in electing tribunes as long as Augustus himself exercised the powers of a *tribunus plebis* every year. For this reason knights were sometimes nominated as tribunes of the people, who did not have to remain in the Senate after their term expired if they did not wish to. In such instances it becomes evident to what extent senators' sense of identity was dictated by the dominant figure of the princeps. Augustus gave an even clearer sign after the death of his son Gaius Caesar when he created, by law, new electoral commissions consisting of senators and knights only, to sift the candidates and choose a list whose election was then a foregone conclusion. The commissions were named after his two deceased sons, Gaius and Lucius, and the candidates were proposed in their names. Augustus could not have indicated any more clearly where political decisions were made, including decisions about the outcome of elections.

The addition of men from new families produced a profound alteration in the Senate during the long decades of Augustus' rule, although it did not mean that the old republican families lost their special status entirely. Augustus attempted to bind as many of them as possible to his own cause permanently, usually by arranging marriages with his own relatives. Quinctilius Varus, who met his end in the forests of Germany, had married into the princeps' clan, as had the Domitii Ahenobarbi, whose last descendant was the emperor Nero. Augustus honored other families by elevating them to patrician status, a right he had acquired through a law passed in 30 BC. A chief function of both old and new patricians was to serve as priests in the state cult, which Augustus had restored in full; according to accepted belief, the rites that they performed guaranteed the continued existence of the *res publica*. The families distinguished in this manner acquired an enhanced social standing, but at the same time the awareness increased that they owed it to Augustus rather than possessing it in their own right. In all these ways, their dependence on him grew.

Augustus introduced further measures with a similarly equivocal effect on the Senate and its power. Early on he had the Senate create a small commission consisting, in addition to Agrippa and himself, of the two consuls, a praetor, a tribune of the people, an aedile, a quaestor, and 15 additional senators. The lower-ranking members changed every six months. Augustus discussed the most important political questions with this small group before they were raised on the floor of the Senate. Being named to this commission no doubt increased some members' sense of their own importance. On the other hand, the rapid rotation naturally reduced an individual senator's significance compared to that of the two permanent members, Augustus and Agrippa. Furthermore the overall effect of the commission's preliminary deliberations was to lower the level of energy invested in the plenary sessions, and the members of the commission who also belonged to the Senate were more or less bound to support the commission's conclusions, meaning in most cases the views of Augustus himself. A similar effect was achieved by shortening consuls' terms and thus increasing the number elected during each year. From 5 BC on, the two consuls who began their term on the first of January tended to be replaced before the year was out, usually on the first of July. This measure permitted twice the number of senators to hold the highest office of the republic; afterwards they enjoyed the prestige of consular status both in the Senate itself and in Roman society for the rest of their careers. But since each consul's term of office was simultaneously reduced by half, it effectively lessened the amount of power he could wield. Of course no one foresaw the development that would take place under Caligula (AD 37–41) and Claudius (AD 41–54), when two and three pairs of suffect consuls would serve terms of only three or four months each year. But the measures introduced by Augustus initiated the process that would ultimately drain the consulship of meaningful political influence.

It is not at all certain that Augustus intended such an effect when he permitted the consuls' terms to be shortened; perhaps he raised the number of consulships in response to considerable pressure from many senators. But in any case the loss of effective power in the cases of individual magistrates was offset by other measures that increased the authority of the Senate as a whole. The most obvious instance is the gradual expansion of the Senate's functions to include serving as a trial court in cases of major political crimes and in all criminal cases involving members of the Senate itself. In 2 BC the behavior of Augustus' daughter Julia unleashed a political scandal involving several young senators from extremely influential families. The full background of this affair remains murky, but one group was obviously able to present the matter, in which political intrigue and sex were inextricably entwined, as a conspiracy against Augustus. Quite apart from all the political dangers the scandal threatened, it was especially embarrassing to Augustus, who had backed laws placing particularly heavy penalties on the crime of adultery. Julia's provocative behavior represented a very public disavowal of his own policies. Therefore, although he could have dealt with the charges against his daughter as a private family matter, he brought the case before the Senate instead. Of course the sentence they imposed on Julia was in accord with his own wishes. The senators also tried and sentenced the "co-conspirators." These cases, and several others that went to the Senate although they could have been heard by regular courts, established a precedent by which the Senate could hand down legal judgments, without the necessity of passing a law specifically enabling it to do so. As a result the Senate's powers were significantly expanded. To be sure, under Augustus' successor Tiberius it became evident that senators could never exercise their judicial function without regard for politics. For all its loss of power and dependence on the princeps, the Senate remained a political body, making an impartial dispensation of justice impossible.

In all the policies Augustus adopted regarding the Senate, one of his concerns was presumably always how to put the position and power he had achieved for himself and his family on a permanent footing. He certainly did not intend to achieve this goal chiefly by weakening the Senate and the various senatorial officeholders; rather he needed to ensure that the real decision-making power remained in his hands, either through changing the law or reorganizing the practical machinery of government. It is striking that Augustus left all truly powerful positions both in Rome itself and in the provinces in the hands of senators. All except one of the provincial governors in charge of legions came from the ranks of the Senate; the only exception was the prefect of Egypt, who commanded three legions to start with, and later only two. The Egyptian prefecture was established in 30 BC, however, before the political situation became stabilized, and under Augustus it did not really become a model. We find prefects from the equestrian order in some regions of the empire, such as Asturia in northern Spain, Moesia on the lower Danube, and Judaea, but they were in fact not true provincial governors. Instead they had more dependent roles, administrating smaller territories under the oversight of senatorial governors. The prefect of Judaea, for example, reported to the consular legate of Syria, while the prefect of Asturia ranked below the governor of Hispania Tarraconensis in the chain of command. Thus they cannot be regarded as exceptions to the rule that all military command rested ultimately in the hands of governors chosen from the ranks of the Senate. In addition the commanding officers of the legions stationed in the provinces were young senators. The tradition of granting both political and military authority to men of senatorial rank – and such men alone – was so well established that it did not occur to Augustus to tamper with it. And finally, since almost all of his important political and military associates were senators, any radical change would have reduced their status immediately, and was for that reason unthinkable.

In sum then, under Augustus virtually all the men who occupied positions of power and responsibility in politics, the army, and government administration were at the same time members of the Senate, just as they had been under the republic. All the conditions were thus fulfilled for the Senate to maintain its role as the center of political power, yet, paradoxically, the opposite occurred. After the late 20s BC the Senate ceased to be the body that initiated policy; the impulses that shaped politics no longer originated within it. The reason was that competition for political leadership among senators had all but died out. Rival candidates no longer challenged each another in the public arena, seeking the power to put their ideas into practice. Augustus now occupied the sole center of power, and all the senators took their orientation from him. During the decade following the battle of Actium, many of the older senators could recall the active and vigorous Senate they had known in the later years of the republic. However they also remembered the consequences of their rivalries and disputes and the rifts that had resulted, namely the civil wars and their atrocities. Most of them were worn out and had no desire to continue the battle. As time passed, and the rolls contained fewer and fewer survivors of the old days, the majority of senators had no direct experience of a *res publica* without a princeps at its head. He was the center, for senators as well as the general public. In a decree from AD 20, only seven years after Augustus' death, the senators referred quite matter-of-factly to Tiberius as *princeps noster*, "our leader," by which they meant the leader of the Senate as well as the state. Even during the late years of Augustus' rule, the great majority of Senate members would probably have accepted the same characterization of Augustus.

10

The Practical Implementation of Political Power: Governing the Empire

The political order that began in 28–27 BC – and continued to develop – also determined the policies for administering the far-flung Roman empire. Augustus' appeals to the republican past and his interest in a smooth transition permitted no radical departures from traditional forms of government. Furthermore, Augustus and his contemporaries were under no pressure to introduce fundamental changes. Thus he did not develop a concept with far-reaching organizational consequences for the entire system in the early years, although modern historians have not infrequently credited him with doing so. Certainly by the end of his reign, after 40 years of rule, many innovations had been introduced, but they were developed very gradually, often when situations arose in which it became evident that the old ways would no longer work. Though the political revolution was relatively rapid and thorough, no analogous rapid reorganization of administrative structures occurred.

This relative stability is most clearly apparent in Rome itself, where by the end of Augustus' reign much had changed, but only slowly. The sheer size of the city and its population – which certainly numbered far over half a million at this time – meant that the government faced daily problems on a vast scale. Some of the mechanisms for dealing with them had obvious flaws. Among the serious problems at the start of Augustus' rule were crime, fires, and devastating floods when the Tiber overflowed its banks. But perhaps the most urgent need was for a long-term, well organized system to supply the capital with food. Pompey had shown it was possible to manage effectively the importation of supplies, grain being the most important, but his model had disappeared with its inventor's death. The hunger revolts that occurred during the triumvirate apparently did not prompt Octavian to seek a new solution, and even when a desperate shortage of grain occurred again in 22 BC and the population forced Augustus to take over direct responsibility for food supplies (the *cura annonae*), he did not consider re-organizing the system itself as far as we know. Instead he apparently used ad hoc measures and his own funds to alleviate the worst of the existing famine. He supplied free grain to the people, appointing senators to oversee the process of distribution. But these new officials had no responsibility for assuring continued supply from abroad. This was the crux of the problem. It was not until more than 30 years later, when a protracted food shortage led to mass expulsions of foreigners from the city and nearly brought the government to a standstill, that Augustus decided – in AD 8 at the earliest – to appoint a prefect to take charge of procuring food supplies on a permanent basis, a *praefectus annonae*. The task of this official, who belonged to the equestrian rather than the senatorial order, was to organize imports, chiefly grain, from the provinces. He in turn had nothing to do with the distribution of supplies once they reached Rome itself. At the time the grain prefecture was created, no one could foresee how much power the holder of the office would one day possess.

It took about the same length of time for Augustus to create a permanent and effective force to fight the fires that were constantly breaking out in the city. From about 21 BC on he experimented with a troop of some 600 slaves as fire-fighters, an idea proposed by the ambitious Egnatius Rufus during his term as aedile. This force, rather small for a city the size of Rome, was at first under the command of the aediles, and later under the *vicomagistri*, the four representatives of each district in the city. Only when Egnatius Rufus' plan proved inadequate did Augustus establish seven cohorts of 500 (or 1,000) firemen. Each cohort was responsible for protecting two of the 14 large sectors into which the city was divided. The prefect in charge of the Roman fire brigade was also appointed from the equestrian order, not to take power away from the Senate, but because the prefect's duties were considered beneath the dignity of a senator. Once established in AD 6, the Roman fire brigade continued to exist on this basis for several centuries.

Other areas of municipal government developed in a similarly gradual manner. After serving as aedile, Agrippa continued to maintain the water-supply system as a private citizen at his own expense. After his death in 12 BC, Augustus had the Senate choose three of its members to serve as the first public commissioners for the water supply and to ensure that the aqueducts did not fall into disrepair. A further commission of five senators was created to maintain public buildings and the temples of the state cult. Called the *curatores locorum publicorum iudicandorum*, they were also empowered to determine which lands were public property. This group came into existence quite late in Augustus' rule and did not oversee building construction; the commissioners were not responsible for the celebrated architectural transformation of Rome in the Augustan era (see chapter 13). Another late innovation was the creation of a city prefecture as a permanent office; the prefect's chief duties were to maintain public order, especially among slaves, and to hear cases of freedmen and other members of the lower social orders accused of crimes, so that justice could be swiftly dispensed. He also supervised three cohorts of 500 men who functioned as a police force. The Praetorian Guard came to play a role in public safety in Rome only later, during the reign of Tiberius, when the guardsmen were moved into barracks on the Esquiline Hill. Under Augustus they were stationed mainly in towns around Italy, and were not a conspicuous presence in Rome itself.

The rest of Italy remained virtually unaffected by administrative reforms. The approximately 400 Italian towns and cities in the heartland of the empire were responsible for all the problems of their citizens, in which the princeps and the central government did not intervene as a rule. Although Augustus divided Italy into eleven regions, from Lucania-Apulia in the South to Venetia et Histria in the North, they do not seem to have played any permanent role in his government. As far as we know they served as administrative units only for the registration of state-owned land and the census. Lists of citizens were always organized by region. The regions themselves had no permanent officials, for that would have run counter to republican tradition. As Romans saw it, the tasks regional officials might have carried out belonged to the magistrates, in particular the praetors. Only in one Italian domain did Augustus see a need to act, and that was the system of long-distance communication. To maintain his political and military ascendancy he needed to keep abreast of developments throughout the empire, and for the information to reach Rome with enough speed for him to react effectively, he needed good roads. Thus as soon as he had established his authority on a firm basis Augustus set about repairing old roads and building new ones. At first he followed the republican tradition, initiating and financing single projects himself, but he also tried to persuade leading senators to invest their spoils from successful military campaigns in extending the Italian network of roads. This attempt proved a failure, and so in 20 BC Augustus took over direct responsibility for roads, the *cura viarum*, with the result that he had to spend far greater sums than before. His donations to the public treasury, the *aerarium Saturni*, for road construction were publicized on coins in 16 BC. Since he needed ongoing oversight, he created through a Senate decree another group whose members, the *curatores viarum*, kept track of the state of the roads. Like the *curatores locorum publicorum*, the senators in this group did not constitute a public building authority; they had to work through local officials and contractors to organize regular repairs.

Through these measures Augustus created the infrastructure that made it possible to reach all parts of Italy and the provinces to the north, and to send and receive information without undue delay. To improve it still further, he added a system of relay stations, where couriers and other government officials could change horses and chariots, or spend the night at the station's hostel. Within Italy this system was organized and run by an experienced army man called *praefectus vehiculorum*, the prefect of vehicles. The government did not actually provide either the chariots or the horses, however; it was the duty of local town magistrates to ensure that there was always a sufficient supply of both. Nor was the system free for those using it; officials were supposed to pay for services at fixed rates. Nevertheless, the potential for abuse was present from the beginning, for how could town magistrates protest if a powerful proconsul, en route to his province with his retinue, forcefully demanded more horses than he was entitled to by the regulations? Yet it is important to note that under Augustus such costs were not simply transferred to adjacent towns in Italy – or in the provinces where the system was also established – as a disguised extra tax. Augustus had a good sense for how much people would be able to endure after the excesses and destruction of the recent civil wars. His promise to look after the inhabitants of Italy and the provinces was not just a political slogan.

On the other hand the promise did not translate, either in the Italian heartland of the empire or in the provinces, into an administrative network without gaps, much less a clearly and efficiently organized government bureaucracy. In the provinces, the existing system established during the republican era, which gave governors extensive power over subject peoples, remained in place in principle; the changes introduced by Augustus were far more political than administrative in nature. Proconsuls selected from the Senate ranks by lot were sent to govern the provinces of the Roman people. They served one-year terms which could be extended if necessary, and occasionally such extensions were granted. At first the number of proconsular provinces varied, and what became the standard number of ten was not arrived at until very late in Augustus' reign, in the first decade of the new era. The proconsular governors were not dependent on Augustus in terms of law, nor was their independent military command taken from them, despite occasional assertions to the contrary by modern historians. In practice, however, the proconsuls could not do much with their independence, since toward the end of the Augustan age Africa was the only remaining province with a legion stationed in it. They retained a few auxiliary troops, but that was all.

In all other provinces Augustus was the legal governor after 27 BC; from 23 BC on his *imperium* as proconsul provided the legal basis for his authority. Since he could obviously not personally govern all the provinces assigned to him – their number rose from five in 27 BC to about 13 at the end of his reign – representatives acted in his stead. They were known as *legati Augusti pro praetore*, legates of Augustus with the rank of praetor. The term reflects the legal and political hierarchy of power clearly, as the legates' title includes the name of their superior, Augustus, and gives them a rank below his proconsulship. Augustus alone decided who would represent him in a particular province, and for how long. As a general rule the legates served longer than the proconsuls, but we cannot say whether the term of three years, which became the average for a legate in the first century AD, was already the norm under Augustus. Many factors contributing to the three-year average had not yet come into play.

Legates and proconsuls had the same powers in their provinces, with one major exception. Each proconsul was responsible, with his quaestor, for collecting regular property and poll taxes. From the start, however, Augustus' legates apparently did not receive this authority, for no quaestors were sent to their provinces. From the time of Sulla on the regulations stipulated that 20 quaestors were to be elected annually. This number would have been insufficient for the increased number of provinces, but electing more would have conflicted with Augustus' claims to have restored the republic. Augustus therefore named agents, called procurators, to supervise the collecting of taxes in his provinces for him. He borrowed this model from the world of commerce, and consequently the procurators acted at first as Augustus' personal emissaries. They performed no public functions and could not be regarded as officials, since they were responsible solely to Augustus. The subordinate nature of the position meant that senators, the members of the actual political class, could not hold it; thus in the main procurators came from the equestrian order. In the early years Augustus sometimes appointed his own freedmen, including the notorious Licinus, whose "unconventional" methods in Gaul brought the princeps huge cash reserves. But since after a short time the procurators' activities came to resemble those of magistrates closely, it became politically disadvantageous to have freedmen serving in that capacity. From then on Augustus appointed only Romans of equestrian – meaning free-born – rank as procurators, at least on the provincial level. The procurators' staffs, by contrast, were recruited at first entirely from Augustus' own freedmen and slaves.

This reapportionment of authority for taxes has often been viewed as an important instance of political progress in the Augustan age, because it put an end to the exploitation of the provinces through tax collection by private contractors, which had been the norm in the republican era. Some historians seem to have equated the abolition of the republican abuses with the modern notion of direct tax collection by government officials. Yet as we have seen, this is not entirely accurate. Neither the quaestor nor the procurator of a province was in a position to levy taxes directly from the population, as they lacked the network of offices and numerous subordinates that would have been necessary to carry out such a task. Instead taxes were usually collected on the town or tribal level, either by municipal magistrates or private contractors. Augustus could in fact not afford to give up the old system for gathering tax revenues, and he had no reason to replace it. What did disappear was the influence of the tax-collection corporations, whose financial power was so great during the late republic that they controlled the votes of many politicians and could influence political decisions to their own advantage. Some corporations went out of business, while the others were forced to accommodate their operations to the new system. Among other things this meant that they had to reduce their profits to a level where the inhabitants of the province in which they operated would not be raising loud protests of exploitation in Rome too often. In Augustus those subjects had a political patron whose duty it was to take care of the entire empire, and who would not ignore disturbances in subject territories for the sake of tax contractors' profits. The same holds for the senatorial proconsular governors and their opportunities for exploitation. While Augustus could not treat them as his direct subordinates, he could exert influence, and if a conflict arose, the interests of a whole provincial town would probably take priority over his sense of loyalty toward one senator. Augustus' political patronage in this sense offered the provinces protection from excessive demands, and is the real cause behind the decisive transformation of the administrative system.

11
A Standing Army

The *Res Gestae* begins with a programmatic sentence. "At the age of nineteen," Augustus wrote, "by my own decision and at my own expense, I raised an army, with which I freed the republic oppressed by the tyranny of a faction." It is the clearest possible identification of the source of his power and the basis on which he maintained it – namely the army.

The Roman republic would not have come to an end if the army had not become a factor in domestic politics. Political power in Rome was distributed among the leaders of the different parties, and so when they fell out with one another in the late republic the army splintered into forces backing each of them. Only when Rome and the political leadership were reunited could the factional forces coalesce and become the Roman army again. This step was achieved after the battle of Actium. But Augustus' aim had to be the establishment of lasting bonds with the army; the legitimacy of his claims to political supremacy rested on his success in ending the civil wars, and keeping the army under control was the only way to banish the threat of another civil war. Augustus certainly never considered returning the army to its old basis under the republic, as a militia of rotating recruits, each of whom spent only a short time in military service; that would have destroyed the basis of his own power. Augustus thus became the actual founder of a standing army. That it would exist was a foregone conclusion; all that remained was to determine what size army the empire and its inhabitants would accept, particularly in terms of cost.

At the time of the battle of Actium the two opponents appear to have commanded more than 60 legions between them, in addition to auxiliary cohorts, most of which had been provided and financed by dependent tribes and client kings. The Roman legions of both sides became the responsibility of the victor. Many soldiers with long years of service behind them were expecting their discharge, and Octavian dissolved entire units in order to reduce the numbers to what he regarded as necessary – and affordable. We do not know on what he based his calculations. Presumably Agrippa had a decisive influence on the final decisions. In the end, 26 legions were retained, to which two more were added a few years later, when the kingdom of Galatia was declared a Roman province. The army remained at this strength for the remainder of Augustus' rule. Soon, however, auxiliary units of 500 men were created in addition to the legions. These troops were usually recruited from defeated peoples immediately after their conquest, including the Asturians in northern Spain, the Breucians of Pannonia, and the tribesman of Raetia, north of the Alps. Such transfers weakened the enemy's strength and at the same time they added to Rome's military potential. In addition, regular contingents from allied tribes like the Batavians and the Ubii played a significant role. The tribes supplied the number of soldiers stipulated in their alliance treaties, and these contingents were not officially counted as part of the Roman army. They were commanded by their own officers and paid for by their tribes, but in Roman currency. If large amounts of Batavian or Ubian coins have been found, especially in the camp at Beckinghausen used by the Romans during their offensive in the area, this has nothing to do with pay for the soldiers. Obviously the auxiliary cohorts supplied by allies were under the orders of Roman commanders in any military engagements.

The total strength of the armed forces stationed in the provinces cannot be precisely determined. The 28 legions had a target strength of 170,000 men, but the number of auxiliary troops in the provinces early in Augustus' rule is unknown. We do know that at least 80 auxiliary units fought on the Roman side in the rebellions in Pannonia between AD 6 and 9. But even if their strength in the early days was roughly equivalent to that of the legions, the army's total numbers would still have been relatively modest given the size of the empire. Nonetheless the financial burden on the state treasury was enormous. While we have no precise figures for treasury receipts from taxes, customs duties, and tributes paid by client rulers, it is certain that the majority of it went to the army. Even so Augustus had to resort to emergency measures to finance all of the military's needs. The base pay of a legionary was 900 sesterces per year. Even if the entire army had consisted solely of enlisted men, their annual pay would then have amounted to at least 140 million sesterces. But in fact the figure was far higher, since the cavalry were better paid and the higher ranks of centurions, tribunes, and legionary legates earned enormous sums compared with ordinary infantrymen. On top of that came the costs for equipment, constructing camps, and maintaining the fleets in Italy and in the provinces, as well as the nine cohorts of the Praetorian Guard and the three urban cohorts, who received higher pay. As time passed the Roman budget also had to cover more and more of the costs for auxiliary troops. And finally, on occasion Augustus paid special bounties to army units or even the entire army. In his will he stipulated that 1,000 sesterces should go to each praetorian, 500 to each member of the urban cohorts, and 300 to each legionary. This one-time payment, which amounted to more than 50 million sesterces, was paid out of his personal fortune, just as during his lifetime Augustus had sometimes used large amounts of his own money for the army. In several instances he personally bought the land on which veterans were settled, paying a total of 600 million sesterces in Italy and 260 million in the provinces. In chapter 16 of the *Res Gestae* he stresses the fact that there was no precedent for such a practice. His aim in mentioning it was to distance himself from Sulla, but also from his own earlier practice of settling veterans on land expropriated from Roman citizens, who received no compensation. Augustus does not mention that land was sometimes seized from conquered peoples in the provinces in order to pay off veterans.

Nevertheless it would be a mistake to assume that Augustus paid most of the day-to-day expenses for the army out of his own pocket. Even though his income was enormous, it would not have been sufficient. He was able to spend "private" funds for the veterans' settlements in Italy and elsewhere at certain times only because war booty was considered his personal property. The running costs for maintaining the army were paid from the state treasury (*aerarium Saturni*), into which all state income, including taxes from Augustus' own provinces, was declared to flow for legal and accounting purposes. Soldiers' discharge bounties were also supposed to come from the state treasury. Probably from AD 5 on, every legionary received 12,000 sesterces at the end of his service, and a praetorian received 20,000. Although we do not know how many soldiers from the legions and praetorian cohorts reached the end of their term of service and became eligible for discharge bounties, the total must have come to at least 50 million sesterces, and was probably far higher.

As soon as Augustus shifted the basis of the veterans' discharge bounties from land grants to cash payments – a step that seems to have occurred in 13 BC – he faced the problem of liquidity. Most importantly, the soldiers had to be given the impression, at least in public pronouncements, that payment of the expected discharge bounties was secure. This very question had often been the subject of political disputes in the late republic. Because the Senate had usually refused to make the necessary provisions, first the veterans and then the soldiers on active duty became the instruments of their commanders in the political struggle to get what had been promised to them. Augustus had to prevent such dangerous discontent from arising again. He experimented with various approaches; in the years 7 BC, 6 BC, and 4–2 BC he paid the discharge bounties from his own inheritance, hardly a permanent solution. The answer was finally found in AD 6, when a general financial crisis had made more demands on the state treasury than usual. With the reforms he introduced at this time Augustus made it clear that his solicitude as ruler could no longer be limited to the concerns of Roman citizens; he also had to take into account the limits of what could be squeezed out of subject peoples. And it was they who bore the costs for the standing army, since Roman citizens in Italy, and also in the colonies which both Julius Caesar and Augustus had founded in the provinces for veterans and landless Italic peoples, paid no regular taxes.

Should these conquered peoples now pay to support the veterans of the legions in their old age as well, when the soldiers were all Roman citizens? Augustus decided against such a solution and demanded that the senators, who as Roman citizens paid no taxes themselves, devise a way for Romans to share in the costs of defense both at home and abroad. When the Senate failed to come up with a realistic proposal, Augustus carried out a plan of his own. He imposed a five-percent tax on all inheritances and bequests, known as the *vicesima hereditatium*. Small legacies to close relatives remained tax free, but larger bequests, which members of the upper classes traditionally made to numerous friends and clients, became taxable as a rule. In order to convince property-conscious Romans that it was for a good cause, Augustus created a separate treasury, the *aerarium militare*, or "military chest." Despite its name, however, the money did not go to finance the standing army, which continued to be paid out of the state treasury, but only to support veterans. The three senators named to serve as prefects of the military fund were dependent on Augustus, at least in practice if not theory, as it was he who made the first deposit of 170 million sesterces to start the fund going. Augustus made a point of mentioning it in chapter 17 of the *Res Gestae*. He did not ask for or accept contributions from others, suggesting that he was keenly aware of the propaganda effect his gesture would have on the troops.

To be sure, the army itself had to pay a share of costs for the veterans, too. After Augustus had fixed the terms of service of the praetorians at 12 years and of the legionaries at 16 years, making them shorter than before, he let them stand for about two decades. Then, however, as he was seeking a financially stable arrangement in AD 5, he extended them again, to 16 and 20 years respectively. Furthermore the soldiers did not receive a full discharge at the end of this term, but had to serve in an emergency reserve for several more years. When Augustus died in AD 14, troops stationed on the Lower Rhine and in Dalmatia mutinied, protesting that after being forced to serve for 30 or 40 years, legionaries were still not allowed to go home, but had to continue serving in special units. Some of these complaints were exaggerations, but the deep-seated resentment had arisen from concrete causes. It had apparently not been possible to make the soldiers understand the overall situation, particularly the shortage of cash to pay their discharge bounties. They made their contributions to the total financing of the armed forces – through postponement of their discharge – as unwillingly as the senators paid their own share in the form of inheritance taxes.

Despite all the imperfections of the system, Augustus nevertheless made an effort to meet soldiers' expectations of a fixed term of service with a reliable financial settlement at the end of it. Mutinies were thus rare during his reign. In one such case, when soldiers who had experienced the civil wars mutinied in Spain in 19 BC, Agrippa gave them dishonorable discharges, meaning that they received no bounty. Politically this was possible because Augustus had no rivals left who could or would have exploited the soldiers' discontent for their own purposes.

Augustus was not the commander-in-chief of the entire Roman army. Legally, as we have seen, a proconsul in one of the provinces of the Roman people was an independent commander of the troops stationed there. Tiberius, Augustus' successor, once found it necessary to remind a proconsul of Africa, for instance, that the proconsul, as governor, was responsible for distributing medals and decorations to the troops in his province and did not need to ask permission from the princeps. As this case reflects, the overall supremacy of the princeps developed more from the political subservience of the senators than from any legal reforms. Of course even in military matters Augustus could impose his will on proconsuls on the basis of his *imperium maius*, his higher authority, but only in cases of conflicting opinion. His *imperium* was not conceived as a blanket supreme command. Sometimes a proconsul could be placed under Augustus' *auspicia* or command, as in the case of Cornelius Lentulus, who as proconsul of Africa between AD 6 and 8 finished a war against the Gaetulian tribe on this legal footing. Passage of a special decree by the Senate had been necessary to create it, however. Normally the *auspicia* were the particular prerogative of a proconsul. Even the right to a triumph was never taken away by legal decree from senatorial commanders who had their own *imperium*; this right was instead allowed to lapse and substitutes were introduced instead. When a senator won a victory after this time, he did so as the princeps' legate. If Augustus considered that a particular victory merited a triumph and accepted acclamation as a commander, then on the basis of a Senate decree he could award the triumphal insignia to the successful field commander and thus allow him to share public recognition for the victory. The actual victor received another reward in the form of a bronze statue in the Forum of Augustus in the center of Rome (see above page 62).

In practice Augustus thus had the entire Roman army effectively under his control. In almost all provinces it was also formally under his command, after the proconsul in Illyricum was replaced by a legate of Augustus and after the legions were withdrawn from the province of Macedonia, which continued under the rule of a proconsul. He appointed his legates as well as the commanders of the various legions; their powers were derived from the *imperium* of the princeps. This fact affected the attitudes of both the commanders and their men, who knew that the powerful senator at the head of the provincial army was himself dependent on the princeps. Moreover some of the centurions and many tribunes owed their position in the army to Augustus' influence. All of them had sworn an oath to him, which they renewed every year. Both centurions and tribunes in particular received generous pay, and these circumstances, in addition to the prospect of further promotion, created a strong network of loyalty to the *imperator*, in which the senatorial legate was also bound. Augustus made great demands on his troops; the wars of conquest in Spain, the Balkans, and Germany required enormous efforts and caused heavy losses. But for many soldiers the memories of battle and its hardships may have soon paled beside their pride in what they had achieved under Augustus' leadership. Numerous inscriptions on graves and the pedestals of honorary statues show that contemporaries were kept informed of the military honors he had awarded. And every award also testified to the victories won by Caesar Augustus.

12

War and Peace: Expanding the Empire

Augustus made it emphatically clear that he wanted his name to be associated with victory. As noted earlier, *virtus* – military courage and valor – was one of his four virtues recognized by official decree of the Senate in 27 BC (see page 3), and in fact his very name implied triumph after he adopted *Imperator*, a word meaning "victorious commander," as his first name. His list of titles included mention of how many times he had been acclaimed *imperator* by his troops on the battlefield and had accepted the honor. By AD 13 the total had reached 21. It reflects how often Augustus could have entered Rome in a triumphal procession if he had wanted. No Roman before him had achieved comparable success, either in this area or in the number of times he had "modestly" declined triumphal honors awarded to him. Virtually the whole of chapter four of the *Res Gestae* is devoted to his victories and military honors.

All of this goes hand in hand with his claim to have brought peace to Rome. He intended his rule to go down in history as the *pax Augusta*. The altar of Augustan peace, the *ara Pacis Augustae*, which the Senate voted to build in 13 BC on Augustus' return from Spain and Gaul, represents one public demonstration of this intention; another is the three times he closed the shrine of Janus Quirinus. This was supposed to occur only when peace reigned everywhere the Romans governed – a peace, it was always implied, achieved by victorious Roman troops. Augustus stressed in chapter 13 of the *Res Gestae* that before his own time this had happened only twice, whereas it occurred three times during his own rule.

In actual fact these claims of peace applied mainly to the situation within the empire; outside its borders no Roman before Augustus waged as many wars successfully, although these wars also cost Rome heavy losses. Under his more than 40-year rule Rome gained more territory than in any comparable period of its prior history. He added northern Spain, the Alpine regions of Raetia and Noricum, Illyricum and Pannonia, and the entire region north of Achaea and Macedonia as far as the Danube to the empire. In Asia Minor part of Pontus, Paphlagonia, Galatia, and Cilicia became provinces, and Judaea was added to the province of Syria. Egypt had already been placed under the government of the Roman people in 30 BC. In addition the borders of the province of Africa were extended to both the east and the south. Thus in almost every region around the entire Mediterranean basin Augustus expanded the area of Roman supremacy, justifying his assertion in chapter 26 of the *Res Gestae* that he had enlarged the area of all those provinces on whose borders there had lived tribes still independent of Rome.

Not all the territorial expansion of the period resulted from military campaigns. After King Amyntas of Galatia died, the region was converted into a province in 25 BC without any need for a concerted military effort. And when King Herod's successor Archelaus became embroiled in a dangerous conflict with his subjects in his realm of Judaea in AD 6, Augustus deposed him. Judaea was attached to Syria and placed under a prefect from the equestrian order, who acted as regional governor. A census then being conducted in Syria therefore also included the inhabitants of Judaea. This is the "taxing of

Cyrenius" (Quirinius) mentioned in the Gospel of St. Luke in connection with the birth of Jesus.

In most cases, however, the methods by which the empire was enlarged were not quite so peaceful. In this Augustus followed the example of the great generals of the republic, although unlike them he was able to mobilize the military potential of the entire empire for his battles. Most importantly, because he remained in power for so many years he could develop long-term strategies and attempt to carry them out. Augustus' policy of military conquest was also fundamentally in tune with public opinion, since for centuries Romans had regarded an expansionist course at the cost of others as not just their right, but almost a duty. Virgil's pronouncement that the gods had granted the city on the Tiber sovereignty without limit, an *imperium sine fine*, does not express merely the poet's personal opinion; it reflects an inner conviction prevalent throughout Rome's ruling class. They favored expansion, and Augustus could rely on their support for such a program. Yet even if the public confronted him with no difficulties of a general kind, a particular goal might well arouse opposition in some quarters. Many people clearly thought efforts to expand the empire should be concentrated in the East, a world that had fascinated people since the time of Alexander. This fascination increased after Sulla and Pompey returned from their campaigns in the region with so much interesting booty. Moreover Roman pride had suffered no small blow from its defeats at the hands of the Parthians, first in Crassus' fiasco at Carrhae, and then when Antony suffered heavy losses and had to retreat in 36 BC. Romans remained painfully aware that the enemy still possessed Crassus' captured battle standards. They craved revenge and the restoration of their honor.

Julius Caesar had been planning a campaign against the Parthians when he was assassinated, but Augustus did not follow his example. We do not know the precise reasons for his decision, but the notion that peace was a preferable alternative to expansion certainly played no role in his thinking. It is probable that he regarded Rome as the center of the empire, and the region beyond the Euphrates may well have seemed just too distant. And perhaps he took the earlier defeats so seriously that he decided not to risk a large-scale campaign against such a great power as Parthia. In this instance he disappointed public opinion. To protect the empire's eastern flanks Augustus relied first of all on client kings with whom he created ties to Rome; they secured the borders with their own troops. He also used diplomatic negotiations on several occasions, but kept a Roman army stationed in Syria, just in case. In 20 BC Augustus employed a tactic that proved effective for a considerable time. It consisted of traveling to the East and remaining there, while his stepson Tiberius undertook the actual negotiating with the Parthians. After Tiberius managed to obtain the return of the battle standards, symbolically so important, they were able to use this success to maximum effect on the home front. In Rome the Senate and people erected an arch in the Forum Romanum that depicted not only Augustus in a triumphal chariot, but also the rescued standards. When the temple of Mars Ultor was completed in the Forum of Augustus, the emblems themselves were placed for safekeeping in the temple's inner shrine. Augustus intended the temple as a center for all cult rites connected with military campaigns; the statues of victorious commanders were placed there, and it was made the site of Senate votes on war and peace. Hence the diplomatic success achieved with the Parthians was presented at home in thoroughly military images, thereby fulfilling Romans' expectations at least in part.

The genuine theaters of war were located in the West, chiefly along the Rhine and the Danube. There victories alternated with defeats, as new territory was conquered and then lost again. But on the whole the balance lay on the side of victory.

Soon after completing the major steps in restoring the republic in 27 BC, Augustus went to Spain. During the preceding decade Asturia and Cantabria in northern and northwestern Spain had been the scene of repeated fighting. Some of the governors had been able to celebrate triumphs at home, but none of them had achieved lasting domination over the rebellious tribes. That the situation was serious enough to require Augustus' personal intervention, however, seems rather unlikely. It is more probable that, after carrying out his domestic reforms, he wanted to demonstrate his concern for the provinces (see above, pages 53–54). An unusually large force, consisting of at least seven legions, was assembled in northwestern Spain. Even though Augustus announced quite soon thereafter that the Cantabrians had been defeated, the fighting actually continued until 19 BC; during its final phase Agrippa took over the command. The newly acquired territories became parts of two provinces, Lusitania and Hispania Tarraconensis, that Augustus already controlled, meaning that they remained under his leadership. One important result of the campaign was acquisition of the mineral deposits and mines in northwestern Spain. The riches derived from them were immediately invested in other campaigns for conquest.

As soon as the campaigns in Spain ended, a good number of the legions that had fought there were transferred to Gaul. Presumably they were required there – in addition to the inhabitants of the province – to build roads in the network Agrippa was extending from Lugdunum (present-day Lyon) to the Rhine and the English Channel. The regions east of the Rhine, from its upper course to the North Sea, had clearly begun to interest the group of leaders close to Augustus. This is suggested not only by their road-building projects, but also by the construction of a camp for legionaries at Dangstetten just north of the Rhine near Waldshut, and the resettlement of the Ubian tribe in the years 19–18 BC. The Ubians were moved from the area near the Celtic-Germanic ring fort at

Dünsberg (on the River Lahn east of the Rhine) to the fruit-
ful but then almost unpopulated low-lying area known as the
Cologne Basin, further down the Rhine. Ubian coins found
there, which were minted between about 20 and 10 BC, indicate the date of the resettlement. The intention was to have
the Ubians, who were allies, act as a buffer and protect Roman
Gaul from raids by other, restless Germanic tribes attracted
by the province's riches. We cannot know for sure what
concept Augustus and Agrippa had developed for the region
of Germania east of the Rhine at that time. However, it
appears to have involved the idea of an offensive campaign
from the beginning. When in 16 BC the Germanic tribes of
the Sugambri, Usipeti, and Tencteri inflicted heavy losses on
M. Lollius, Augustus' legate, and even captured one legion's
eagle standard, the defeat seems not to have led to the for-
mulation of new plans, but only to have strengthened the
Romans' already existing intention to wage a large-scale war
of conquest in the region. They had incorporated the kingdom
of Noricum in the eastern Alps into the empire that same year.
Noricum became part of the province of Pannonia and was
probably ruled by a prefect from the order of knights, who
reported to the senator serving as governor of Illyricum/
Pannonia (which was later made into two separate provinces).
This is the model also used in Judaea in AD 6. A year after
Noricum was absorbed, Augustus' stepsons Tiberius and Drusus
conquered the adjoining part of the Alps to the west, which
later became the province of Raetia. For the first time Italy's
own borders did not adjoin territories controlled by unsubdued tribes. The recently conquered region now surrounded
the core territory of Roman citizens like a protective arch.
The success of the campaign was considered so important
that the poet Horace included a literary memorial to the
victory in the fourth book of his *Odes*. For Augustus himself
the Senate erected only a few years later the *tropaeum Alpium*
(trophy of the Alps) at La Turbie, as an enormous monument

to victory on a hill near Monaco. Still visible as a ruin today, it was intended to glorify the incorporation of the peoples of the Alps into the Roman empire.

It is hardly possible to separate the conquest of the Alps and their northern slopes from the two offensives begun in 12 BC, by Drusus against the Germanic peoples east of the Rhine and by Tiberius against the Pannonian tribes in Illyricum. In both cases the campaigns may have been prompted by the fact that the traditional homelands of these tribes straddled the frontier of the empire. The unsubdued groups just beyond the frontier represented a continuing potential of unrest for the border provinces, and the Roman aim was probably to prevent uprisings before they could occur. Augustus and Agrippa may have been pursuing large-scale strategic goals as well, but ancient records provide no information on that subject.

Tiberius succeeded in subduing most of the Illyrian and Pannonian tribes in a four-year war; smaller campaigns followed in the next few years. The region clearly did not prove very difficult for the Romans to conquer. The resistance was small, and presumably the different tribes fought separately rather than joining forces against the aggressors. The relative ease of conquest led the Roman leadership to misjudge the tribes' willingness to live in peace under their rule. Fifteen years later this nearly lead to a catastrophe for the occupying forces.

Drusus did well in Germania, too, achieving territorial gains quickly. The fact that he was not merely conducting punitive raids is shown by the existence of several early camps on the River Lippe, such as Oberaden or the supply fort Beckinghausen, both of which were built to enable troops to remain in the region over the winter. In 9 BC Drusus reached the River Elbe, having subdued a large portion of the German tribes. When Drusus fell from his horse on the march back and died of his injuries, Tiberius took over his command. After the field campaign of 8 BC the historian Velleius Paterculus could claim that Tiberius had very nearly made Germania into a tribute-paying province. Even though the author, who had served under Tiberius, intended his history as a tribute to his former commander, this statement probably comes close to the truth. In any event, the Romans continued expanding their presence in the region, and they left their military camps and bases as visible – indeed almost monumental – signs of their intention to remain. Camp Haltern on the Lippe was built on such a scale that it must almost have resembled a fortified city, and Waldgirmes in the Lahn valley, conceived as a civilian settlement from the beginning, even had stone buildings. If Roman rule in the region had lasted longer, a greater number of such centers would probably have arisen.

Tiberius' withdrawal from politics in 6 BC and his retreat to the Greek island of Rhodes (see below page 117f.) did not cause the Romans to alter their policies toward Germania. Rebellions do seem to have occurred, however. Much remains hazy because of gaps in the historical record, but it is clear that Germania remained firmly in Roman hands until Tiberius returned to the Rhine in AD 5. The task that remained, it appears, was to defeat King Marbod, who had withdrawn to Bohemia with his tribe, the Marcomanni, and from his base there had established a far-reaching system of alliances with other Germanic tribes. The Romans feared he might incite tribes under Roman rule to rebellion, and Tiberius' goal was to eliminate this threat. He planned a campaign that had its main bases at Mainz in upper Germania and Carnuntum in Pannonia. The advance was carefully planned, as is shown by the construction of a large camp at Marktbreit upstream from Mainz on the River Main, even though the camp was never actually used. Twelve legions had already set out when Tiberius received news of an uprising in Pannonia and had to divert his forces; King Marbod's might was never broken by the Romans.

The scale of the threat facing the Romans in Pannonia required Augustus to concentrate all his efforts there. Clearly the Pannonian tribes had joined forces. The challenge to Roman authority appeared so dangerous that Augustus posted guards in the capital itself. New auxiliary units were formed; slaves were called up, and their owners required to free them for military service. Conscription of citizens was ordered as well, even in Rome itself. In the end ten legions and at least 80 auxiliary units were assembled under Tiberius' command, and with them he finally succeeded in crushing the revolt in AD 9. Both sides suffered enormous losses. Despite the victory – and the triumph accorded to Tiberius – the empire had exhausted its financial and military resources. The army and the state treasury both needed some time to recover.

Only a few days after the decree granting Tiberius his triumph had been passed, however, reports of a fresh disaster reached the capital. P. Quinctilius Varus, the governor of Germania, had committed suicide after a battle east of the Rhine, in which the tribal forces had wiped out three of his legions and nine auxiliary units. The enemy leader, a young prince of the Cherusci named Arminius, had served as prefect of an auxiliary troop in the Roman army and, like many Germanic chieftains, had received Roman citizenship as a reward. In return for this distinction, Augustus and his political allies had expected loyalty to Rome. Many tribesmen did remain loyal, but the leaders of the rebellion among the Cherusci and other ethnic groups demanded solidarity against Rome from their peoples. It is a matter of debate whether the revolt occurred mainly among the Germanic auxiliary troops attached to the Roman army, who were of course very well versed in Roman battle tactics, or whether the rebellion had a broader base. But even if the uprising began among the troops, the fact that such a large proportion of the tribal population joined the rebels proved the decisive factor. Varus was apparently too trustful of Arminius and his confederates. Later the Romans accused Varus of having provoked the revolt by his own behavior; he had treated Germania like a province, they said, exacting tribute and administering justice. Varus was certainly entitled to do so, however, for at that time Germania indeed had the status of a province within the Roman empire.

It was apparently a report of an uprising among one of the tribes in late summer of the year AD 9 that persuaded Varus to undertake the expedition resulting in his own death and the destruction of his troops. Arminius and his confederates exploited the rainy weather and their familiarity with the area. Tacitus names as the site of the catastrophe the *saltus Teutoburgiensis*. The present-day Teutoburg Forest southeast of the city of Osnabrück did not receive its name until the early modern period, however, and that hilly region is not the place where the Romans met defeat. In the past decade excavators have discovered near Kalkriese (north of Osnabrück) the remnants of metal fittings from a large number of chariots, arms, and other military equipment, strewn over a distance of several kilometers, along with collapsed ramparts and hastily buried stashes of coins. This new evidence lends support to the view that Varus' army was destroyed here. However, it cannot be considered the site of the battle, for a single battlefield never existed as such. The fighting took place over a considerable distance and lasted for three days; Varus and some of his senior officers committed suicide, and the remaining leaderless troops were captured or massacred by the rebels.

Panic nearly broke out in Rome. But while Romans feared that the Germanic tribes would cross the Rhine and conquer Gaul, their opponents failed to reach agreement on such a plan. King Marbod refused to participate in a joint attack against the Romans, even though Arminius sent him Varus' severed head as an inducement. The situation on the Rhine was tense, but it remained quiet. Scholars have concluded repeatedly that Augustus responded to the disaster with the realization that he would have to alter his policies toward Germania. In fact, however, it appears that he decided to continue his offensive strategy, since he not only replaced the destroyed legions with new units, but even increased the forces stationed along the Rhine. Tiberius, who was again dispatched to the region, immediately led retaliatory raids against the disloyal tribes. Even more importantly, Drusus' son Germanicus took command of the troops on the Rhine front in AD 13 and won a victory that same year, for which Augustus accepted his last acclamation as victor in Germanicus' stead. Augustus' acceptance makes it likely that he had given Germanicus orders to win back the lost territories. And finally, not all of Germania east of the Rhine had rebelled; several tribes on the North Sea coast had remained loyal to Rome. Thus when Augustus wrote in chapter 26 of the *Res Gestae* that he had pacified Spain, Gaul, and Germania from the ocean at Gades to the mouth of the River Elbe, his claim was accurate. It was Tiberius who in effect renounced the policy of expansion in Germania.

Augustus almost overtaxed the capabilities of the empire with his military offensives, and he did not achieve his goals everywhere. He ordered the prefects of Egypt, Aelius Gallus and C. Petronius, to undertake the early campaigns against an Ethiopian kingdom in southern Egypt and against the realm of the Sabaeans at the southeastern end of the Arabian peninsula between 25 and 22 BC. Augustus boasts in the account of his deeds that his troops had advanced further to the south than any Roman army before. Such a claim was flattering to Romans' pride and could increase the prestige of the princeps, but a lasting success there was denied him, just as it was later in Germania. Nor were the frontier disputes with the Parthians ever fully resolved. Some 20 years after the pact of 20 BC Gaius Caesar, Augustus' adopted son, had to be sent once more to pacify the eastern border of the empire, and he, too, failed to achieve a permanent success. More important than this general setback, however, was a wound Gaius Caesar received during a siege, from which he did not recover. His death was a personal catastrophe for Augustus. At the time of the princeps' own death, no lasting solution to the conflict in the East had been found.

However, despite these failures and the costly losses in the areas around the Danube and east of the Rhine, Augustus appeared to the Romans as a great conqueror who had expanded the empire, indeed as the greatest commander in Roman history. The territories of his other successful conquests all remained parts of the empire for many centuries, and testified to the soundness of his policies in Romans' eyes.

13
Rome, the Augustan City

Few of Augustus' successors had as thorough a personal experience of the empire; only Hadrian (117–138) outdid him in the extent of his travels. Even before acquiring supreme power Octavian had seen parts of Italy, Greece, Illyricum, and Sicily, and after the battle of Actium he visited many parts of the East. In the years 21–19 BC Augustus traveled to the East again, while Tiberius negotiated with the Parthians. But he spent even more time in the western provinces, particularly Spain and Gaul. During the years 27–24 BC and 16–13 BC he ruled the empire from there, and his last journeys took him to Gaul twice more, in 11–10 BC and 8 BC. On these travels, a feature developed that was to be characteristic of the Roman monarchy: The center of the empire moved with the ruler. Emissaries from Indian kings sought Augustus out in Tarraco (modern Tarragona) in 25 BC, and on the island of Samos and in Antiochia, Syria, in 20 BC. Ministers of Queen Candace of Ethiopia also arrived in Samos to negotiate a peace treaty. The Senate repeatedly sent small delegations of its members to distant points to confer on political questions with Augustus. Wherever he went, that site became the center of politics and the only place where major political decisions could be made.

In spite of this Rome remained the actual center of power; it would never have crossed Augustus' mind to shift it elsewhere permanently. And this mode of thought, with Rome as the focus, was matched by the princeps' actions. It was Augustus who made the city the architectural centerpiece of the entire empire. From his reign on, the inhabitants of the capital could see the power of the monarchy with their own eyes, for it was now expressed in architectural imagery. The sphere of architecture resembled other areas linked to politics, however, in that it was also necessary to display a certain respect for republican traditions.

One instance is provided by the restraint Augustus showed in not constructing a palace to match his exalted rank. The sumptuous imperial residence whose ruins can be viewed today was constructed by his successors; it was they who transformed the Palatine Hill into the emperors' domain. Augustus himself respected the principle once formulated by Cicero: "The Roman people despise luxury in the private sphere, but appreciate magnificent display in public." While still a triumvir, Octavian acquired a house on the Palatine Hill, where according to legend Romulus had founded the city. With grand political plans in mind, Octavian may have chosen the location expressly for its symbolic associations. The size and style of the house remained relatively modest, however, at least in comparison with the opulence favored by other Roman political leaders during the late republican era. Naturally many symbolic changes were made to the building during Augustus' long life. When the new political order was established in 28–27 BC, the Senate decreed that a laurel tree be planted on each side of the entrance, and that the civic crown, awarded for saving the lives of citizens, be placed above the door. No other Roman aristocrat could boast of a house with these distinctive features.

After his election as *pontifex maximus* in 12 BC, Augustus was unwilling to move into the quarters traditionally inhabited by the high priest. He could not escape the requirement that the priest live in a *domus publica*, a public residence, however, and so the princeps converted one part of his house into a public space. In addition Augustus created a shrine to the goddess Vesta in the house. In the temple of Vesta in the Forum Romanum her priestesses, the Vestal Virgins, guarded her sacred flame; Livia, Augustus' wife, assumed this role in the high priest's residence. In this way the house became a site where public functions and private life were mingled.

The combination of functions found even clearer expression in the architectural features Augustus added to the property. When lightning struck the grounds shortly after Octavian had acquired the house, he declared the spot a sacred precinct, and erected a temple there to Apollo, the god who had protected him. This was the first temple in Rome to be constructed entirely of white marble from Carrara. Later the oracles of the Sibyl would be stored here under the cult statue, and during the Secular Games the temple was the focus of the celebration, at which Horace's *Secular Hymn* was sung. The temple complex included a library and a porticus. As Augustus grew older, the Senate began to meet more and more often on his property; the old republican assembly followed the princeps geographically as well as ideologically, gathering on the hill of Romulus, mythical ancestor of the Julian family.

For his part Augustus transformed the Forum Romanum, the architectural heart of republican Rome. He did not bring this about by commissioning buildings himself, but it was nonetheless Augustus' person, his family, and his ideas that were represented in the new monuments. Officially, the Senate decreed their construction and absorbed some of the cost. But step by step, structures dedicated to the princeps and his relatives were erected in the Forum, so that by the time of his death it had altered its identity and become a center entirely dominated by the Julian family. The first new edifice was the temple of the deified Julius Caesar on the eastern side – the clearest and most ostentatious sign imaginable that a new order had been established. An altar in front of the temple marked the site of Caesar's funeral pyre. After Actium a new speaking platform was erected in front the altar, decorated with the long prows of ships captured in the battle. (These prows, used for ramming enemy vessels, were known as *rostra*, "beaks.") It faced the renovated platform from the republican period on the western side. They represented the two epochs that met there, but victory clearly belonged to the latter era. Next to the Temple of Caesar stood the elaborate Parthian Arch with its three passages; displayed on the attic, or upper level of the arch, were the recovered battle standards together with a statue of Augustus. Beyond it rose the Temple of Castor and Pollux, which dated from the republican era. It was later rebuilt entirely in marble by Tiberius in his own name and that of his brother, Drusus, with the names of the builders proclaimed in enormous bronze letters. Adjoining this structure, which dominated the forum by its sheer size, was the Basilica of Gaius and Lucius Caesar, with a nave and four aisles; it was dedicated to the memory of Augustus' two adopted sons, both of whom died young. The Curia, where the Senate met, was also completely rebuilt and aligned so as to face the Forum. Its new name, the Curia Julia, announced the identity of the renovation's sponsors. In chapter 19 of the *Res Gestae* Augustus placed the Curia first in the list of buildings he had erected in Rome. The Basilica Aemilia was the sole exception to renovations in the name of Augustus or one of his relatives, as the Aemilian family, who had originally constructed it in the second century BC, undertook the work independently. The only truly new construction not associated with the name of Augustus was the paving of the open space in the Forum; this measure, undertaken by the praetor L. Naevius Surdinus, was presumably commissioned by the Senate and paid for with funds from the state treasury. The visual effect and symbolic power of the Forum were created by the Augustan edifices.

Near the Forum Romanum, more and more altered from its appearance in the republican era, the princeps built his own forum to the north of the Curia, from which it was separated only by the Forum of Julius Caesar. "On my own land I erected the Temple of Mars Ultor (Mars the Avenger) and the Forum Augustum from the spoils of war," he reported in chapter 21 of the *Res Gestae*. The temple, which he had vowed to build before the battle of Philippi, became an enormous structure, part of an architectural complex that also served utilitarian functions. However, the building's most important purpose was to create an architectural statement placing the new ruler in a context including the lineage of the Julian family and, more broadly, the rest of Roman history. The architecture presented Augustus as the culmination and fulfillment of both. Mars, father of Romulus, appeared in the center of the pediment, with Venus, ancestress of the Julian family, at his side. In the porticos on both sides of the temple, which stood on a raised podium, the line of descendants was continued from these mythological origins down to the recent past. In the niches of the portico to the left of the temple stood statues of the most important figures in Roman history, starting with Romulus and proceeding to Appius Claudius Caecus, the famous censor, the dictator Sulla, and Julius Caesar's opponent Pompey. Inscriptions attached to their monuments summarized their political and military careers and their acts on behalf of the *res publica*. The sum of their deeds, their own *res gestae*, also led up to Augustus, whose own deeds rested on their achievements but outshone them by far. To the right of the temple the genealogy of the Julian family was represented by a similar series of statues, beginning with Aeneas, the hero of the Trojan War, and ending with Marcellus, Augustus' son-in-law who died young, and the princeps' stepson Drusus. Both lines ended with Augustus himself, whose statue, depicting him driving a chariot, dominated the piazza. The inscription below it praised him as father of the nation. The architectural imagery recast the military ruler as a paternal monarch.

Augustus' transformation of the city of Rome extended far beyond the two centers where he concentrated his monumental self-depiction. The list of his construction or renovation projects contained in chapters 19–21 of the *Res Gestae* is far from complete, but it includes some of the most important temples in Roman history, such as the Capitol, the Temple of Quirinus on the Quirinal Hill, and the Temple of Diana on the Aventine Hill. In the year 28 alone, he reported, under the Senate's authority he rebuilt 82 of the temples that had been allowed to deteriorate during the years of political unrest. By restoring the temples, Octavian underlined for his contemporaries his claims to have restored the republic and refounded the city, like a second Romulus.

The list of secular edifices named by Augustus in the *Res Gestae* is astonishingly short; besides the Curia he mentions the Theater of Pompey, which he rebuilt, and the Theater of Marcellus, constructed in honor of his son-in-law, and the aqueducts that he either had rebuilt or expanded in their capacity. Utilitarian building projects were usually entrusted to Agrippa. Although Agrippa already had consular rank in 33 BC, he served once more as aedile, so as to have an official mandate for overseeing new construction, although he had to use his own funds to pay for it. Even after his term in office Agrippa continued to direct public building for practical needs. Two new aqueducts, the Aqua Virgo and the Aqua Iulia, greatly increased Rome's supply of fresh water. The Aqua Virgo was used mainly for the Baths of Agrippa on the Campus Martius, and for the fountains in the nearby park. Next to the baths stood the Pantheon, where visitors were met by monumental statues of Augustus and Agrippa in the vestibule. Inside statues of the gods awaited them, including one of the deified Julius Caesar. The spheres of human beings and Olympus were connected in the Pantheon, but not mingled.

Agrippa also finished construction of the Saepta Iulia, an enclosure begun by Julius Caesar, who intended it to serve as the site for the assembly of the people; with it he combined a hall where votes were to be counted. The dimensions of the Saepta Iulia were gigantic, and it was opulently decorated with staggering amounts of marble. In political terms, however, these monumental structures were superfluous, magnificent shells with no actual function. The inhabitants of Rome soon took to using them as places to stroll and enjoy themselves – not unimportant amenities in a large city where most people lived in very crowded conditions. Equally important were markets and storehouses like the *macellum Liviae*, a spacious market on the Esquiline Hill, named after Augustus' wife, Livia.

In a little over 40 years the face of Rome was fundamentally transformed, in a manner paralleling the changes in political life. All over the city new structures rose, either commissioned by Augustus or connected with him or members of his family. Everywhere inscriptions announced the names of the princeps, his sons or grandsons, or associates such as Agrippa, whose name can still be made out above the entrance to the Pantheon. In not a few cases they consisted of *litterae aureae*, enormous letters of gilded bronze that glittered in the sunlight on temple architraves, obelisks, or arches and informed the citizens of Rome of the princeps' fame and his deeds. He was also omnipresent in the form of statues – on the speaking platform in the Forum, in front of the Temple of Mars Ultor, in the portico of the Pantheon, and in the chapels erected between 12 and 7 BC in each of the 265 wards of Rome. The cult rites there were devoted chiefly to the Lares, the tutelary deities of the locality; among them a statuette of the genius of Augustus was venerated as the embodiment of the masculine virtue active in him. Augustus himself donated these statuettes to the chapels. Whenever a holiday was celebrated and sacrifices were offered to the local deities, his genius was among the recipients.

Thus the princeps' presence pervaded the public space and life of Rome in a manner impossible to overlook. And the message conveyed by all the public buildings, inscriptions, and statues – which became clearer and clearer with the passage of time – was that Augustus was not only the princeps, the first man among many, but also a monarch, the sole ruler.

14
The Quest for Political Continuity: The Succession

Although Augustus may have ruled alone, there was never an Emperor Augustus. None of his contemporaries could have summed up in a single word what his position really meant. No term existed that included his power, his political possibilities, and at the same time his legal position derived from the "republican" government. Only later generations, who no longer realized how Augustus' position had grown slowly and altered over the course of time, could look back and apply to him such an anachronistic label, "emperor," that drastically misrepresents his actual status. The sum of his power derived first of all from various powers of office delegated to him by the Senate and people, secondly from his immense private fortune, and thirdly from numerous patron–client relationships he established with individuals and groups throughout the empire. All of them taken together formed the basis of his *auctoritas*, which he himself emphasized as the foundation of his political actions. Modern scholars have sometimes taken him too much at his own word.

A position of power assembled from so many different components could not simply be passed on to another person, above all not by Augustus himself. If he had been willing to take such an obviously dictatorial step, he could have done so soon after coming to power, without bothering to build up his position, in a gradual and politically elegant manner, in a government that officially remained a republic. But he wished to preserve the appearance that not he himself was in charge of the Roman state, but rather the Senate and people, in whose hands lay the responsibility for choosing a leader. Persuading the Senate and people to cooperate in this effort was not difficult. But the persuasion had to be brought to bear in a manner that did not contradict the ideology of the restored republic. Augustus proved to be a master in influencing public opinion and especially the Senate as he wished, while still obeying the official rules of the game.

Certainly he never considered allowing his position to come to an end with his death. Like every other Roman aristocrat in the republic, he wished the position he had achieved to be passed down within his own family – in his case a position that meant monarchical leadership of the Roman republic. Thus it is not surprising to find that from the early days of his rule he made efforts to pass his position down within his own family; he just did not say so openly. The problem always consisted for him in the fact that he had no son to whom political offices and family power – meaning money and clients – could be passed on in the way Romans regarded as natural. His only child was his daughter, Julia, born to Scribonia, his second wife, in 39 BC. The course of her life was determined in essential respects by the political goals of her father, and for the same reason it also ended in catastrophe. A long road led to this dreadful end; it was a life that may have looked splendid on the outside, but one in which her personal needs and wishes played virtually no role.

During his sojourn in Spain from 26 to 24 BC, Augustus arranged for her to marry his 17-year-old nephew Marcellus, son of his sister, Octavia. The need to bind Marcellus even more closely to Augustus' own family seemed so urgent that Augustus had the wedding take place in his absence, with

Agrippa standing in for him as father of the bride. As son-in-law of the princeps, Marcellus immediately gained political standing. Nothing reveals this more clearly than testimony from the trial of M. Primus, a former proconsul of Macedonia. In his trial, which probably took place in 23 BC, Primus was accused of having waged a war against the Odrysi outside the frontiers of his own province without having obtained authorization first. In his own defense he claimed that he had indeed received instructions to undertake the campaign – not only from Augustus, but also from Marcellus. Whether his statement was true or false is immaterial for our purposes; what counts is the degree of political influence that people attributed to Marcellus, simply because he was Augustus' closest male relative. It cannot be doubted that the princeps saw in him the man who in the long run would play the decisive role next to him. This never came to pass, however, because Marcellus died before the critical year 23 BC was out.

Before Marcellus' sudden death, Augustus took pains to avoid even the suggestion of a dynastic succession based solely on his own will. Augustus also fell seriously ill in 23 BC, but recovered. Before his recovery rendered the question of his replacement less acute, rumors were rife that he had identified Marcellus as his "successor" in his will. Since the rumors persisted, Augustus finally decided to respond by having his will read aloud in the Senate in order to remove all doubts. The message he intended to send was probably directed less at the general public than at his own party and especially Agrippa, his most important associate. After Marcellus died it was Agrippa who took his place, and again the relationship was cemented by creating a tie to Augustus' immediate family. Agrippa was required to divorce his wife and marry Julia. Agrippa was given his own *imperium* as a proconsul in 23 BC, and five years later was granted the powers of a tribune of the people (*tribunicia potestas*) as well. With these powers he advanced to something like Augustus' own powers in legal terms, although a difference of status between them remained. In 20 BC Julia bore Agrippa a son, and in 17 BC a second son followed. After the second boy was born, Augustus adopted both of them in a public ceremony, turning his grandsons officially into his sons. He introduces Gaius and Lucius Caesar as sons in the *Res Gestae*. From the very beginning the goal he was pursuing with this adoption was clear to all: At some point in the future one or the other would succeed him. The external forms did not even conceal the goal particularly; although he took care that no one could accuse him of violating the laws of the republic. And for the time being the question did not arise, since Agrippa, the real father of both of Augustus' "sons," possessed sufficient authority and legal power in his own name to replace Augustus if necessary. Because the boys who might one day replace Agrippa in the role of successor to Augustus were Agrippa's own sons, no rivalry developed between him and the two young Caesars.

It appeared that Augustus had defused the urgent problem by means of an elegant, two-generation solution, but only five years later, in 12 BC, the dream was shattered. Agrippa died while both of Augustus' grandsons were still minors, too young to exercise any genuine authority. The princeps, too much of a realist not to recognize this, once again sought a solution within his immediate family. When Livia married Octavian she already had two sons, named Tiberius and Drusus, from her first marriage. She had a strong interest in securing positions of power for them, and so we may assume that she influenced her husband when plans for the future had to be revised. Their chief concern was to find another husband for Julia. Drusus, the younger son, was already married to Antonia, Augustus' niece; this relationship was already too much within the family to be disturbed. Tiberius' wife, on the other hand, was "only" Vipsania, a daughter of the late Agrippa from his first marriage. And so Tiberius was forced to divorce her, and marry Julia as soon as her period of mourning for Agrippa ended.

There is considerable evidence that Tiberius consented to the new marriage only under compulsion, bowing to the urgent political necessity, especially since he and Julia were not well matched in character and personality. Of course it is also possible that concealed ambition to occupy the highest position in the republic may have played a role in Tiberius' calculations. Yet in assigning specific powers to Tiberius Augustus acted with far more restraint than he had previously shown toward Agrippa. Tiberius was granted several acclamations as *imperator* (together with Augustus) for the military victories he achieved in Pannonia and Germania. And in 7 BC, during his second consulate, Tiberius even celebrated a triumph over Germania – the first triumphal procession that Augustus had permitted since 19 BC. But it was not until 6 BC that the princeps had the Senate grant him the *tribunicia potestas*, a step that seemed to reveal Augustus' intentions for the future. It was already too late. Before the year was out, Tiberius withdrew from politics and even left Rome. He went to live on the island of Rhodes – as if he had been banished. Although there has been much speculation, we will never know for certain just what happened. It is certain, however, that his disturbed relationship with Julia played a role. There were a great many tales in circulation alleging that she had numerous love affairs with other men, but it is impossible now to determine to what extent they were merely malicious gossip spread by a curious public.

It is probably of more consequence for Tiberius' withdrawal that he had been forced to look on from the sidelines as both of Augustus' "sons" – who were 14 and 11 years old in the year 6 BC – gained more and more prominence. The princeps sponsored games in their names as an occasion for officially presenting them to the people, and the spectators understood the message Augustus wished to send. Both boys also joined colleges of priests at an early age. Two years earlier, in 8 BC, Augustus had taken Gaius Caesar with him to Gaul, in order to introduce him to the army. The legions on the Rhine received a bonus in his name in addition to their regular salary, a tried-and-true method for creating bonds of loyalty. After Tiberius' retreat to Rhodes the picture took on even clearer contours. In 5 BC Augustus accepted the consulate again, in order to give additional splendor to the ceremony in which Gaius reached his majority and put on a man's toga for the first time. The Senate voted to admit Gaius to its deliberations. In the same year he was designated to become consul five years later, when he would be only 20 years old. Rome had never had a consul so young. Gaius' cohort of the equestrian order elected him their leader, the *princeps iuventutis*. No Roman could fail to see the parallel between him and Augustus, who was *princeps senatus*, leader of the Senate. Even the inhabitants of the provinces realized who would hold power in the future and sent envoys to assure the young "prince" of their loyalty. Inscriptions from southern Spain and Asia Minor have revealed that the annual oath sworn to Augustus was expanded there to include Gaius Caesar and his younger brother. When Lucius reached the age of majority in 2 BC he received the same rights and honors as Gaius. Thus Augustus appeared to have doubly secured the transfer of power within his own family, if he could only live long enough to give his successors adequate training. Both young men needed to gain more experience in dealing with the army and governing the provinces. In the year 1 BC Gaius Caesar was dispatched to the East to learn more about the region, to negotiate with the Parthians, and to install a client king in Armenia. He assumed the consulship in Syria in AD 1 and, after capturing the Armenian stronghold of Artagira in AD 3, was acclaimed *imperator*.

At about this time Lucius was supposed to spend some time with the army in Spain, in order to keep pace with Gaius. Upon reaching Massilia (now Marseille) in southern France in AD 2, however, Lucius died suddenly. Augustus had to see one of his promising young sons laid to rest in the mausoleum he had built for himself. The next blow was not long in coming; Gaius suffered a wound during the siege of Artagira from which he did not recover. In February of AD 4 he died in Limyra in Lycia (in southern Turkey) on his way home. Augustus had to open his mausoleum a second time, to bury the ashes of his second son, and with them his hopes for a successor related to him by blood.

Tiberius' moment had come at last. Augustus had long been deaf to Livia's pleas on her son's behalf, but allowed him to return to Rome shortly before Lucius' death. The relationship between the two men had grown more distant since Julia had become the focus of a scandal and Augustus himself had intervened to end Tiberius' marriage to his daughter. Now, after the divorce, they were merely stepfather and stepson. But once Gaius died as well, Augustus was forced to act, and he did so, purposefully and yet with caution. For a short time there was no plan in place in case the princeps should die suddenly. No doubt he was involved in lengthy negotiations – and probably serious arguments – with both Tiberius and Livia, for Augustus still insisted on a long-term solution on his own terms. Although Tiberius had a son of his own, the then 18-year-old Drusus, Augustus demanded that he adopt his nephew Germanicus, his brother Drusus' son, who was only slightly older than Tiberius' son. The probable reason was that through his mother, Antonia, who was Augustus' niece, Germanicus was related by blood to the family of the princeps. Tiberius finally capitulated and adopted Germanicus as his son on June 26 or 27 in AD 4. On the same day or the day after Augustus then adopted Tiberius, making a son out of his stepson and former son-in-law.

That same year Tiberius received all the forms of authority that were necessary to lead the state, including the powers of a tribune and a proconsul. Every acclamation as *imperator* for Augustus was now expanded to include Tiberius as well, and in AD 13 he celebrated his second triumph. In addition, emissaries from foreign kings were required to pay their respects to Tiberius, an unmistakable indicator of his status. And finally in the same year, AD 13, Tiberius received an *imperium* equal to Augustus' own. It empowered him to act in every province, where he could also command the troops. By this time Tiberius was doubtless aware that Augustus had named him as his chief heir in his will, dated April 3, AD 13. In the event of the princeps' death, the legal transfer of power had been arranged. It was also time for Augustus to put the finishing touches on the account of his deeds that had long been in preparation. Between June and August AD 14 he made the last changes in the text. Despite all the setbacks that had occurred, he could look back on a complete and fulfilled life.

15
Augustus' Death and the Future of the Empire

Thoughts of death can never have been far from Augustus' mind. His health was fragile; he had to reckon with the possibility of dying suddenly at a young age. It was for just this reason that he made preparations early on for the time after his death, in an effort to see that no political vacuum arose.

The princeps also prepared his own burial site in advance. As far as we know, he began building his mausoleum on the Campus Martius outside the sacred perimeter of the city in 32 BC, even before his war against Mark Antony had been resolved. Presumably the primary purpose of the action was to make a political point against Antony – namely to demonstrate to the Roman public that Octavian, at least, saw the center of the empire and his own political career in Rome, and wished to be buried there. However, by the time the structure was more or less finished – probably around 28 BC – Octavian had no more Roman rivals for power. The gigantic circular mausoleum became something else, namely the expression in monumental form of the princeps' political ideology and the power of the ruling family.

The mausoleum was the largest that had ever been built in Rome up to that time. Slightly more than 290 feet in diameter, and estimated to have been almost 150 feet tall, it dominated the northern end of the Campus Martius. The white travertine of the circular lower wall contrasted with the evergreen shrubs and trees planted on top of it, surrounding the tumulus or upper level (a cylinder surmounted by a dome). On both sides of the entrance the wall was faced for a distance of about 130 feet with gleaming white marble, as was the front side of the upper cylinder. The first person to be buried there was Augustus' son-in-law, Marcellus, followed by the other members of the family who predeceased Augustus, including Agrippa and his two sons, Gaius and Lucius. Inscriptions summarizing their achievements were added to the ring wall after their deaths, gradually altering its appearance. Two obelisks were placed on the piazza in front of the mausoleum, probably about 11 BC. After the princeps died, two square bronze pillars were added on either side of the door, presenting to visitors the text of the *Res Gestae* on two (or perhaps three) sides.

The character of the mausoleum as a political monument of family rule was enhanced by its architectural and topographical surroundings. Around it Augustus created spacious parks, to encourage the public to come and spend time, during which they could not fail to see the statues and trophies of victory, and their accompanying inscriptions. When the Senate voted the construction of the *Ara Pacis Augusti* (peace altar of Augustus) on the princeps' return from Gaul in 13 BC, the whole precinct south of the mausoleum was redesigned. Part of it was turned into a giant sundial, whose gnomon, or indicator, was the first obelisk brought to Rome from Egypt. (Today the same obelisk stands in front of the Italian parliament building.) Lines to indicate the months of the year, days, and hours were inlaid in bronze in the paving stones of the dial's elliptical face. The dial was oriented so as to place the marble enclosure of the altar directly on the line for the equinoxes, when day and night are of equal length, and on September 23, the day of the autumnal equinox, the shadow of the top of the obelisk fell precisely on the entrance to the altar – pointing to the man to whom the altar had been dedicated. September 23 was also Augustus' birthday. At the very moment of his birth it had been cosmically determined that Augustus would bring peace to the world – after the civil wars and the defeat of Antony and his Egyptian queen. The obelisk, consecrated to the god of the sun, thus also symbolized Octavian's victory over Egypt. The birth, victorious destiny, and death of the princeps were rendered visible in a single enormous monument – thus was his figure to transcend mortality.

By the year AD 13 at the latest, Augustus must have felt his strength waning. He asked the Senate to create a committee of 20 senators with whom he could discuss matters of state; their decisions should be considered equivalent to decrees voted by the full Senate. The state of Augustus' health was also the reason why in that same year Tiberius was granted an *imperium* as comprehensive as Augustus' own. In the summer of AD 14 Tiberius set out to visit the legions in Illyricum, and Augustus accompanied him as far as Beneventum in Samnium and then went on to Nola, the town in Campania where his father had died. He may have consciously chosen to stop there, knowing that the end was approaching. On August 19, AD 14, he died there; tradition says in the same room as his father. Livia was at his side, and Tiberius, the "son" and successor, whom his mother had summoned. The princeps had arranged for the transfer of political power to take place without tumult, and his planning succeeded. Tiberius acceded to the principate, and no one protested.

From Nola a long train of mourners accompanied Augustus' body back to Rome. He had made all the arrangements for his own funeral in advance. On the day of his burial all public and private business came to a standstill, and the inhabitants of Rome and visitors from the provinces by the hundreds of thousands took part in the funeral observances. From his house on the Palatine Hill the magistrates designated to serve in the coming year carried his remains to the Forum Romanum on a bier of gold and ivory. Tiberius and his son Drusus delivered the funeral orations from the two rostra, and then the procession passed through the Porta Triumphalis to the Campus Martius, where a cremation site had been chosen close to the mausoleum. Augustus' coffin, which bore a wax eagle above it visible to all, was placed on the pyre. As the flames rose, an eagle flew up into the sky – a sign that the deceased had been raised to the gods. Later a senator affirmed under oath that he had seen Augustus' spirit rise to heaven. Livia rewarded the witness with the sum of one million sesterces. The Senate proclaimed that Augustus had joined the company of the gods, and was now a *divus*. It voted to begin construction of a temple for his veneration, and to create a new priesthood, the *sodales Augustales*, to celebrate the cult of the deified princeps. Augustus had become a member of the Roman pantheon, a part of the Roman religion and cult on which the future security of the republic depended. Five days after the cremation Livia collected his ashes in a marble urn and placed it in the simple sepulchral chamber at the center of the mausoleum. Above, at the top of the tumulus, from a height of some 130 feet a larger than life-size statue of the restorer of the Roman republic looked down, as if guarding his own work.

That work lasted, even if some modifications naturally occurred with the passage of time. All of Augustus' successors cited his example and claimed him as their model, even when they in fact acted in a very different fashion. They also all adopted his name, *Augustus*. Through this usage it gradually lost its character as a name and became a title. The degree to which Augustus' actions provided impulses for future developments can be seen from the speech that Maecenas, according to Cassius Dio, delivered in 29 BC (see above, pages 41–42). Maecenas' recommendations for how the principate and the empire should evolve are in large measure a summary of what actually ensued in the next two centuries, based on Augustan foundations. In hindsight almost all the notable features of the Roman empire of the first and second centuries were already present under Augustus, if only in outline. Presumably the development could have proceeded along different lines in some areas. But in the main the future was constructed on the basis of Augustus' reign, although he naturally neither foresaw nor planned all that happened. The entire imperial era received its stamp from him without doubt, yet institutions continued to evolve. Even this apparently so conservative epoch is marked by profound change. The same applies to Augustus' own reign. If one dates its commencement from the battle of Actium, it lasted for 45 years. No one ruled the Roman empire longer. However because of the nature of our sources, which were usually written from hindsight, the developments during this long period do not always become clear. Augustus' reign often appears static, just as his portrait, once formed, always displays the same youthful features throughout the decades. There is no portrait of Augustus as an old man.

His actions were at no time uncontroversial, even if no one dared to criticize them publicly from the end of the twenties BC onward. In his *Annals* Tacitus allows both opponents and allies of the princeps to speak at Augustus' funeral, but it is characteristic that even in this sharp characterization the differing judgments are limited almost exclusively to the period of the triumvirate. The accusations raised include cruelty, duplicity, and a craving for power. Even Augustus' most vocal critics could not place his political achievements in doubt, however. He refounded the *res publica* in the form of a monarchy, granted a new political status to the provinces, and achieved a solid peace for most of the empire. None of his successors as ruler of the Roman empire could present a similar balance sheet. And what statesman of later ages could enter into competition with him?

Time Line

63 BC	September 23	Birth of Gaius Octavius, later known as Augustus
59		Death of his father, Gaius Octavius
49–45		Civil war between the parties of Julius Caesar and Pompey
45	autumn	Octavian in Apollonia
44	March 15	Assassination of Julius Caesar; soon thereafter contents of his will made known
44	May 8	Octavian formally accepts Caesar's legacy
43	January 2	Octavian joins Senate and receives propraetorian *imperium*
43	April 21	Battle of Mutina; both consuls killed
43	August 19	Octavian becomes consul
43	November 27	Triumvirate begins
42	October 23	Battle of Philippi; Octavian defeats Caesar's assassins
40		Fall of Perusia; Treaty of Brundisium
39		Treaty of Misenum
38	January 17	Octavian marries Livia

37	autumn	Renewal of the triumvirate according to the Treaty of Tarentum
36	September 3	Defeat of Sextus Pompeius at Naulochos
37–33		Antony's campaigns against the Parthians and Armenians
35–33		Octavian's campaigns in Illyricum
32		Inhabitants of Italy and western provinces swear oath to Octavian
31	September 2	Battle of Actium; defeat of Antony and Cleopatra
30	August 1	Fall of Alexandria
29	August 13–15	Octavian celebrates threefold triumph in Rome
28		Census and purge of the Senate
27	January 13	Octavian returns, in a final step, power to the Senate and people
	January 16	Octavian receives some provinces for 10 years; is awarded name "*Augustus*"
27–25		Sojourns in Gaul and Spain
23		Conspiracy against Augustus in Rome; he resigns consulate, receives tribunician powers, acts as proconsul in his provinces; his *imperium* is effectively extended to all provinces (*maius*)
		Agrippa receives the *imperium* of a proconsul for five years
22–19		Augustus visits the East
21		Agrippa marries Augustus' daughter, Julia
20		Parthians return captured Roman battle standards

19		Augustus' *imperium* is extended to Rome and Italy
18		Agrippa receives tribunician powers
17		Augustus adopts Gaius and Lucius Caesar
17	May–June	Secular Games
16		Lollius defeated; Augustus reorganizes administration of Gaul
13	July 4	Augustus returns to Rome; construction of the *Ara Pacis* decreed
12		Augustus elected *pontifex maximus*; death of Agrippa
12–9		Drusus' campaign against the Germanic tribes east of the Rhine; Tiberius conquers Pannonia
11		Tiberius and Julia marry
9	January 30	Dedication of the *Ara Pacis*
9		Drusus dies in Germania
8		The month of *Sextilis* is renamed *Augustus*
8–7		Tiberius' campaign in Germania
6		Tiberius receives *tribunicia potestas*; he withdraws to Rhodes
5		Gaius Caesar dons the *toga virilis*
2	February 5	Augustus receives the title *pater patriae*
AD 2		Tiberius returns from Rhodes
2	August 20	Lucius Caesar dies in Massilia
4	February 21	Gaius Caesar dies in Limyra
4	June 26–27	Augustus adopts Tiberius following Tiberius' adoption of Germanicus; Tiberius receives the *imperium* of a proconsul and the *tribunicia potestas*
6–9		Rebellion in Pannonia

9		Roman army in Germania is destroyed; death of Varus
10–12		Tiberius' second campaign in Germania
13		Last renewal of Augustus' and Tiberius' *imperium*
13	April 3	Augustus writes his will; Germanicus in Germany with his own *imperium*; acclamation as *imperator*
14	May	Augustus and Tiberius complete the census; last revision of the *Res Gestae*
14	August 19	Death of Augustus in Nola
14	September 17	Senate decrees Augustus' deification: *Divus Augustus*

Appendix: The Res Gestae of Augustus

Augustus wrote an account of his deeds and his achievements for the Roman people early in his career. He wanted to show how important his actions had been for Rome and how he deserved recognition for them from Romans. The author revised this report for the last time in the year AD 14. After his death the Vestal Virgins, in whose safekeeping the document had been placed together with Augustus' will, presented it to the Senate. The latter voted to display Augustus' account, the *index rerum a se gestarum*, on two bronze pillars in front of his mausoleum, as the deceased had directed. The depressions in the ground where both pillars stood can be seen today outside the mausoleum immediately to the left and right of the entrance; they were discovered during excavation by Edmund Buchner only a short while ago. The two pillars themselves are lost.

The Senate also had the text of the *Res Gestae* sent to all Roman provinces, in order to make its contents known there. How this was accomplished in every case we do not know, but in one province, namely Galatia in the heart of present-day Turkey, the governor apparently urged the leading families of the province strongly to anchor this "political testament" of the late Augustus in the memories of the province's population "for ever." In the conditions of the ancient world this could only mean that the text should be engraved or carved in stone or bronze, so that the written words would survive the passage of time. The governor's "suggestion" must have been so clear that a whole series of towns in his province carried it out; we know of Ancyra, the capital of Galatia, where the governor also had his seat; Apollonia, a Greek city, and Antiochia, a Roman colony in Galatia that had been founded by Augustus himself. In all three towns the text was published, but not in the same way. This was mainly due to the fact that the original was composed in the Latin language, which the majority of Galatia's inhabitants did not know; the language they generally used in the public sphere was Greek. In Ancyra the text was published in both languages, in the anteroom and on the outer walls of the temple in the city dedicated to the goddess Roma and to Augustus. The temple with the large bilingual inscription is a symbol, as it were, of the encounter and coexistence of the Greek and Roman worlds. In Apollonia, on the other hand, the authorities published only the Greek text, placing it on a large foundation on which stood statues of the deified Augustus and his family. Finally, in Antiochia, the Roman colony, only the original Latin text was published; today it is not known where the inscription was originally placed. It may have been on an honorary arch for Augustus or on the pedestal of an equestrian statue of the princeps. However, in all three cases the text was connected with a visible monument for the deified Augustus.

None of the three inscriptions is preserved in its entirety; there are gaps in all of them. The most complete is the text in Ancyra, and for this reason the *Res Gestae* are often still referred to today as the Monumentum Ancyranum. If we combine the evidence offered by the three inscriptions, then the full text can be reconstructed. This is to say that we have in our hands essentially the text that Augustus himself authorized. It was in this way that he wished posterity to see his achievements for Rome and the Romans.

The *Res Gestae* are of course not an objective text; rather they offer the very personal viewpoint of the author. Nor do they present a full account of events in the years between 44 BC, the year of Caesar's murder, in which Augustus – still known as C. Octavius – first strode on the political stage, and the year AD 14, when the founder of the new form of government, the principate, died. Instead Augustus presents only matters relating to himself: his political and financial achievements and expenses, and the awards and honors he received for them from the Senate and People. The history of this period as seen through Augustus' eyes is one-sided; many events are also placed in a false light, and nowhere does he mention his opponents by name. Nevertheless it is not possible to prove that Augustus made any direct false statements. If one wants to acquire a more comprehensive picture of the Augustan age, including other perspectives, then it is necessary to draw on statements by Greek and Latin authors, on other inscriptions, and papyri and coins, as well as the surviving monuments and visual depictions. This has been done in the present account of Augustus, as the text makes evident again and again. Yet despite the variety of other evidence, the *Res Gestae* must stand at the center of every examination and portrayal of the Augustan age.

Repeated attempts have been made to determine the particular literary form of the *Res Gestae*, but in the end all of them failed. There is no clear and unambiguous model for the work. Instead Augustus, who refers to himself in the first person, created an independent type of self-depiction that had not existed previously. None of his successors is known to have written anything similar to it. Thus the *Res Gestae* appear to be a completely independent and unique work. They should be read as such.

The Res Gestae *of Augustus by Sarolta A. Takács*

The Accomplishments of the Deified Augustus*

Below is placed a copy of the accomplishments of the Deified Augustus[1] by which he made the entire world subject to the power (*imperium*)[2] of the Roman people, and of the expenses, which he incurred for the republic and the Roman people, as engraved on two bronze pillars set up in Rome.

1

At nineteen years of age, by my own decision and at my own expense, I raised an army, with which I freed the republic oppressed by the tyranny of a faction. For this reason the senate enrolled me among its ranks, with honorific decrees, in the consulship of Gaius Pansa and Aulus Hirtius [43 BC], awarding me consular rank for the purpose of voicing my opinion, and gave me *imperium*.[3] It ordered me as *propraetor*, together with the consuls, to see to it that the republic

---

* In this translation I have tried to follow Augustus' syntax as much as possible. When it seemed necessary to translate terms within the text, I have done so by adding them in parentheses. Square brackets indicate additions that are not part of the Latin or Greek text.

suffered no harm. In the same year, the people, however, elected me consul, when both consuls had fallen in battle, and appointed me triumvir to set the republic in order.[4]

2

Those who murdered my father I drove into exile and avenged their crime through lawful legal proceedings. And, afterwards, when they waged war against the state, I defeated them in battle twice.

3

I waged many wars on land and on sea, against internal and external foes, throughout the whole world and as victor, I spared all citizens who asked for forgiveness. Foreign people to whom pardon could be securely given, I wished to spare rather than destroy. About five hundred thousand soldiers were under a military oath of allegiance to me. More than three hundred thousand from those I have settled in colonies or I sent back to their municipalities[5] after their military service. I have assigned all of them land or given them money as compensation for their military service. I have captured six hundred ships, not counting those that were smaller than a trireme.

4

I celebrated two ovations and three curule triumphs, and I was acclaimed imperator twenty-one times.[6] When the senate decreed more triumphs for me, I declined them all. I deposited in the Capitol the laurel with which my fasces were wreathed[7] fulfilling the vows that I had made in each war. For campaigns led successfully by me or my legates under my auspices on land or on sea, the senate decreed supplication for the immortal gods fifty-five times. The days, however, on which supplication was given, by the decree of the senate, were eight hundred and ninety. In my triumphs, nine kings and children of kings were led before my chariot. As I am writing this, I have been consul thirteen times and was in the thirty-seventh year of tribunician power.[8]

5

The dictatorship was granted to me, both in my absence and in my presence, by the people as well as the senate in the consulship of Marcus Marcellus and Lucius Arruntius [22 BC], [but] I did not accept it. I did not beg to be excused, however, from the administration of the grain-supply when there was the worst shortage of food, which I administered in such a way that I liberated the whole city (Rome) from immediate fear and present danger by my expenditures and care in the space of a few days. Then, I also did not accept the offer to hold the consulship yearly and in perpetuity.

6

In the consulship of Marcus Vinicius and Quintus Lucretius [19 BC] and afterward in the consulship of Publius Lentulus and Gnaeus Lentulus [18 BC] and for the third time in the consulship of Paullus Fabius Maximus and Quintus Tubero [11 BC], the senate and the Roman people being in agreement that I alone should be made the guardian of laws and morals with supreme power, I did not accept any magistracy, which was contrary to the customs of our ancestors. Matters that the senate wanted me to conduct at that time, I accomplished through tribunician power; in this power I have, on my own accord, asked for and received a colleague from the senate five times.

7

I was a member of the triumvirate to set the republic in order for ten consecutive years. I was the head of the senate[9] for forty years right up to the day I was writing this. I was *pontifex maximus*, augur, a member of the college of fifteen, a member of the college of seven in charge of public festivals, one of the Arval Brethren, a *sodalis Titius* and a fetial.[10]

8

I increased the number of patricians by the order of the people and the senate in my fifth consulship [29 BC]. I revised the membership of the senate three times. I had a census of the people taken in my sixth consulship [28 BC] together with my colleague, Marcus Agrippa. I performed a *lustrum*[11] after forty-two years. At this *lustrum*, four million and sixty-three thousand Roman citizens were recorded. Then again, acting alone on account of my consular power, I had a census taken in the consulship of Gaius Censorinus and Gaius Asinius [8 BC]. At this *lustrum*, four million two hundred thirty-three thousand Roman citizens were recorded. And then a third time, acting on account of my consular power with my son Tiberius Caesar as colleague, I had a census taken in the consulship of Sextus Pompeius and Sextus Appuleius [14 AD]. At this *lustrum*, four million nine hundred thirty-seven thousand Roman citizens were recorded. By new laws, passed on my advice, I have revived many exemplary practices of our ancestors, which in our age were about to fade away, and myself transmitted to posterity many models of conduct to be imitated.

9

The senate decreed that vows for my health are to be undertaken by consuls and priests every fifth year. In fulfillment of these vows, games were often celebrated in my lifetime, sometimes by the four most prominent colleges of priests,[12] sometimes by consuls. Further, all citizens, either privately or on behalf of their municipalities, have unanimously and continuously made propitiatory offerings for my health at all *pulvinaria*.[13]

10

By a decree of the senate, my name was included in the song of the *Salii*,[14] and it was enacted by law that I should be sacrosanct forever and that I should hold tribunician power as long as I live. When the people granted me the priesthood, which my father had held, I rejected the idea to become *pontifex maximus* in the place of a colleague as long as he was alive.[15] Some years later, after the death of the one who had seized it at the occasion of civil unrest, I received this priesthood in the consulship of Publius Sulpicius and Gaius Valgius [12 BC], and from all of Italy such a multitude, which has never been recorded at Rome before that time, poured in to my election.

11

The senate consecrated the altar of *Fortuna Redux* (Fortune the Home-Bringer) before the temple of Honor and Virtue at the Capena Gate,[16] and it ordered that the priests (*pontifices*) and the Vestal Virgins[17] were to give yearly sacrifice on that day [12 October] when I returned from Syria in the consulship of Quintus Lucretius and Marcus Vinicius [19 BC], and it named the day *Augustalia* derived from my cognomen.

12

At that time, by decree of the senate, a part of the praetors and tribunes of the people together with the consul Quintus Lucretius and the leading men were sent to Campania[18] to meet me, an honor that up to this day has not been bestowed on anyone except me. When I returned from Spain and Gaul, after successfully having taken care of the affairs in these provinces, the senate decreed, in the consulship of Tiberius Nero and Publius Quintilius [13 BC], that an altar of Augustan Peace should be consecrated next to the Field of Mars in honor of my return and ordered that the magistrates and priests and Vestal Virgins should perform annual sacrifices there.

13

The doorway of Janus Quirinus, which our ancestors wanted to be closed when peace on land and on sea was secured by victories throughout the whole empire of the Roman people, and from the time of the city's foundation until before my birth tradition records that it was only shut twice; [however,] when I was the leading citizen the senate ordered it shut three times.

14

My sons, Gaius and Lucius Caesar, whom fortune snatched from me in their youth, were, for the sake of my honor, designated by the senate and the people as consuls when they were in their fifteenth year that they should enter the magistracy after five years. And the senate decreed that from the day they were led into the forum they should partake in public deliberations. All Roman knights also presented each one of them with silver shields and spears and hailed them leader of the youth.[19]

15

In accordance with the testament of my father, I paid each member of the Roman plebs[20] 300 sesterces and in my name I gave 400 sesterces each from the booty of war in my fifth consulship [29 BC]; again also in my tenth consulship [24 BC] I gave each man 400 sesterces from my patrimony, and in my eleventh consulship [23 BC] I bought grain with my own money and distributed twelve rations per person. And, in my twelfth year holding tribunician power [11 BC], I gave every man 400 sesterces for the third time. My largesse never reached fewer than 250,000 men. In the eighteenth year of my tribunician power and my twelfth consulship [5 BC], I gave 60 denarii [240 sesterces] a person to 320,000 members of the urban plebs. In my fifth consulship [29 BC], I gave 1,000 sesterces from booty to every one of my soldiers settled as colonists; at the time of my triumph about 120,000 men in the colonies received this largess. In my thirteenth consulship [2 BC], I gave each member of the plebs, who was receiving public grain, 60 denarii [240 sesterces] a person; they made up a few more than 200,000 persons.[21]

16

I paid money to the municipalities for arable land, which I assigned to soldiers in my fourth consulship [30 BC] and later in the consulship of Marcus Crassus and Gnaeus Lentulus Augur [14 BC]. This sum came to about 600,000,000 sesterces paid for land in Italy and almost 260,000,000 sesterces for provincial land. In the recollection of my generation, I was the first and only one who founded military colonies in Italy or in the provinces to have done this. And afterwards, in the consulship of Tiberius Nero and Gnaeus Piso [7 BC], and again in the consulship of Gaius Antistius and Decimus Laelius [6 BC], of Gaius Calvisius and Lucius Pasienus [4 BC], of Lucius Lentulus and Marcus Messalla [3 BC], of Lucius Caninius and Quintus Fabricius [2 BC], I paid monetary compensation to soldiers I led back to their municipalities after completion of their service, on this account I spent almost 400,000,000 sesterces.

17

I assisted the public treasury with my own money four times, in such a way that I transferred 150,000,000 sesterces to those who administer the treasury. And in the consulship of Marcus Lepidus and Lucius Arruntius [6 AD], when the military treasury was founded on my advice for the purpose of paying compensation to soldiers, who have served twenty or more years, I transferred 170,000,000 sesterces from my own patrimony.

18

From the year in which Gnaeus and Publius Lentulus held the consulship onward [18 BC], when the revenue in kind fell short, I gave out allocations of grain and money from my own granaries and money from my patrimony, sometimes to 100,000 persons, sometimes to many more.

19

I built the *curia* (senate-house) and the Chalcidicum (a court-yard) next to it, and the temple to Apollo on the Palatine with its porticoes, the temple of the deified Julius, the Lupercal, the portico by the *circus Flaminius*, which I permitted to be called after the name of the one who put up the previous portico on the same site, Octavia, a *pulvinar* at the circus Maximus, temples on the Capitol to Jupiter Feretrius (the Smiter) and Jupiter Tonans (the Thunderer), a temple to Quirinus, temples to Minerva and Iuno Regina (Queen) and Jupiter Libertas (Freedom) on the Aventine, a temple to the Lares on top of the *via Sacra* (Sacred Way), a temple to the Di Penates in the Velia, a temple of *Iuventas* (Youth), a temple to Mater Magna (Great Mother) on the Palatine.[22]

20

I restored the Capitol and the theater of Pompey, both works at great expense without putting my own name in an inscription on either. I restored the watercourse of the aqueducts, which in many places were falling apart due to age, and I doubled the water supply from a new spring into the aqueduct called Marcia. I finished the *forum Iulium* and the basilica between the temple of Castor and the temple of Saturn, which were begun and almost finished by my father, and when the same basilica was consumed by fire, I began to rebuild it on a larger site; I began work on it in the name of my sons, and in the case I should not complete it while alive, I have given orders to have it completed by my heirs. In my sixth consulship [28 BC], I restored eighty-two temples of the gods in the city by the authority of the senate, omitting none that required restoration at that time. In my seventh consulship [27 BC], I restored the *via Flaminia* from the city (Rome) to Arminium [Rimini] together with all bridges except the Mulvian and the Minucian.[23]

21

On private ground from booty, I built the temple to Mars Ultor (Avenger) and the *forum Augustum*. On ground that I bought, for the most part, from private owners, I built a theater next to the temple of Apollo, which should be called after Marcus Marcellus, my son-in-law. Gifts from booty I dedicated in the Capitol and in the temple of the deified Caesar and in the temple of Apollo and in the temple of Vesta and in the temple of Mars Ultor, they cost me about 100,000,000 sesterces. In my fifth consulship [29 BC], I remitted 35,000 pounds of gold for crowns contributed by municipalities and colonies of Italy to my triumphs, and later, whenever I was proclaimed *imperator*, I did not accept the gold for crowns, which the municipalities and colonies continued to decree as kindly as before.

22

I gave gladiatorial games three times in my name and five times in the name of my sons and grandsons, at these combat shows some 10,000 men did battle to the death.[24] I presented to the people spectacles of athletes summoned from everywhere twice in my own name and a third time in the name of my grandson. I presented games in my own name four times, and in place of other magistrates twenty-three times.[25] On behalf of the college of fifteen men, as its president (*magister*), with Marcus Agrippa as colleague, I presented the Secular Games in the consulship of Gaius Furnius and Gaius Silanus [17 BC]. In my thirteenth consulship [2 BC], I was the first to present games for Mars,[26] which, afterwards in each succeeding year, have been presented by the consuls in accordance with a decree of the senate and a law. I put up hunts of African beasts for the people in my own name or in that of my sons and grandsons in the circus or the forum or the amphitheater twenty-six times, during which about 3,500 animals were killed.

23

I presented a naval battle across the Tiber as a spectacle for the people at a place now occupied by the Grove of the Caesars, where a site 1,800 feet long and 1,200 feet wide was excavated.[27] There, thirty beaked triremes or biremes, and also many smaller vessels, were set against each other. Besides the rowers, about 3,000 men fought in these fleets.

24

In the temples of all the cities of the province of Asia I as victor replaced all ornaments, which the one against whom I fought had appropriated into his private possession after despoiling the temples.[28] About eighty silver statues of me on foot or on horse or in chariots had been set up in the city (Rome), which I myself removed and with the money from them I set up golden offerings in the temple of Apollo in my name and in the names of those who had honored me with the statues.

25

I wrested control of the sea from pirates.[29] In that war I captured slaves who had escaped from their masters and taken up arms against the republic, almost 30,000 captured ones I handed over to masters for the purpose of exacting punishment. All of Italy took an oath of allegiance to me, and demanded me as their leader in the war, in which I was successful at Actium. The provinces of Gaul, Spain, Africa, Sicily, and Sardinia swore the same allegiance. There were more than 700 senators who served under my standards then, of those eighty-three have been consuls, either before or after – up to the day of writing this – and about hundred and seventy priests.

26

I enlarged the territory of all provinces of the Roman people on whose borders were people who were not yet subject to our *imperium*. I pacified the provinces of Gaul and Spain as well as Germany, which includes the Ocean from Cadiz to the mouth of the river Elbe. I pacified the Alps from the region which is closest to the Adriatic to the Tuscan sea[30] without waging an unjust war on any people. My fleet navigated through the Ocean from the mouth of the Rhine eastward to the borders of the Cimbri, an area no Roman has traveled to before this time either by land or by sea; and, the Cimbri and Charydes and Semnones and other German peoples of that region, through their legates, sought my friendship and that of Roman people. Following my order and under my auspices two armies were led into Ethiopia and Arabia, which is called Eudaimon (Arabia Felix), almost at the same time, great forces of both peoples were cut down in battle and many towns captured. An advance was made in Ethiopia as far as the town of Nabata, which is next to Meroë; in Arabia the army advanced into the territory of the Sabaeans to the town of Mariba.[31]

27

I added Egypt to the empire of the Roman people. After Artaxes had been killed, I could have made Greater Armenia a province, but I preferred, following the example of our ancestors to hand over the kingdom to Tigranes, son of king Artavasdes and grandson of the king Tigranes; Tiberius Nero, who was my stepson then, carried this out. When the same people later revolted and rebelled, I subdued them through my son Gaius and handed them over to the king Ariobarzanes, son of Artabazus, king of the Medes, and after his death to his son Artavasdes; when he was killed, I sent Tigranes, who was from the royal Armenian family, to that kingdom. I recovered all provinces from the Adriatic sea toward the east, and Cyrene, which for a greater part was already in the possession of kings,[32] and, previously, I recovered Sicily and Sardinia, which had been seized in a slave war.[33]

28

I founded colonies for soldiers [who had been released from military service] in Africa, Sicily, Macedonia, both Spains, Achaia, Asia, Syria, Gallia Narbonensis, Pisidia. Italy also has twenty-eight colonies founded by my authority, which, in my lifetime, were very populous and busy.

29

After defeating enemies, I recovered from Spain and Gaul and from the Dalmatians several military standards, which were lost by other commanders. I compelled the Parthians to restore the spoils and the standards of three Roman legions to me[34] and to ask as suppliants the friendship of the Roman people. Those standards, moreover, I placed in the innermost part, which is in the temple of Mars Ultor.

30

The peoples of Pannonia, whom the army of the Roman people never approached before I was *princeps*, were conquered by Tiberius Nero, who was then my stepson and legate;[35] I subjected them to the *imperium* of the Roman people and I extended the borders of Illyricum up to the bank of the river Danube. When an army of Dacians crossed [the Danube] into our side, it was defeated under my auspices and later on my army crossed the Danube[36] and compelled the Dacian peoples to submit to the commands (*imperia*) of the Roman people.

31

Embassies of kings from India, not seen with any Roman commander before, were often sent to me. The Bastarnae, Scythians, and the kings of the Sarmatians, who live on this side of the river Tanais[37] and beyond, the king[s][38] of the

Albanians and the Iberians and the Medes sent ambassadors to seek our friendship.

32

The kings of the Parthians, Tiridates and afterwards Phrates, the son of king Phrates, Artavasdes of the Medes, Artaxares of the Adiabenians, Dumnobellaunus and Tincommius of the Britons, Maelo of the Sugambrians, . . . rus[39] of the Marcomani [and] Suebians, sought refuge with me as suppliants. King of the Parthians, Phrates, the son of Orodes, sent all his sons and grandsons to me in Italy, not because he had been overcome in war but because he sought our friendship by pledging his children. During my principate, many other peoples, with whom no exchange of embassies and friendship existed before, have experienced the trust of the Roman people.

33

The peoples of the Parthians and of the Medes received kings, whom they had sought, through ambassadors, leaders of these peoples, from me: The Parthians, Venones, the son of King Phrates, grandson of king Orodes, the Medes, Ariobarzanes, son of king Artavasdes, grandson of king Ariobarzanes.

34

In my sixth and seventh consulship [28 and 27 BC], after I had extinguished civil wars, when I obtained control of all affairs by universal consent, I transferred the republic from my power to the control of the senate and the Roman people.[40] For this my service I was named Augustus by decree of the senate and the door-posts of my house were publicly wrapped with laurel garlands and a civic crown[41] was placed above my door and a golden shield was placed in the *curia Iulia*, which, as is attested by an inscription on this shield, was given to me by the senate and the Roman people on account of my virtue, clemency and justice, and piety. After this time, I surpassed all in authority, however, I did not have more power than others who were colleagues with me in each magistracy.

35

When I held my thirteenth consulship [2 BC], the senate and the equestrian order as well as the whole of the Roman people named me father of the country and decreed that this was to be inscribed in the vestibule of my house and in the *curia Iulia* and the *forum Augustum* below the chariot which had been set up in my honor by a decree of the senate. When I wrote this, I was in my seventy-sixth year [13 AD].

Appendix[42]

1

All the money he gave either to the treasury or the Roman plebs or to discharged soldiers: six hundred million denarii.[43]

2

The new works were the temple of Mars, Jupiter Tonans and Jupiter Feretrius, Apollo, deified Julius, Quirinus, Minerva, Iuno Regina, Jupiter Libertas, Lares, Di Penates, Iuventas, Mater Magna, Lupercal, the *pulvinar* by the circus, the *curia* with the Chalcidicum, the *forum Augustum*, the *basilica Iulia*, the theater of Marcellus, the *porticus Octavia*, the grove of Caesar across the Tiber.

3

He restored the Capitol and sacred buildings eighty-two in number, the theater of Pompey, the aqueducts, the *via Flaminia*.

4

The expenditure he invested in scenic shows and gladiatorial games and athletic contests and hunts and sea battles and dona-tives to colonies, municipalities destroyed by earthquakes and fire or money to individual friends and senators, whose money-qualification he brought up to full strength,[44] was innumerable.

Notes

1 This passage was at the end of the letter that was sent to the provinces together with the *res gestae* (the accomplishments) of Augustus.

2 The Latin word is *imperium*, which translates to supreme military power, supreme authority. The plural form is *imperia*. The two magistracies that held this power were the consul- and the praetorship. An *imperium* could, as in this case, be given to a senator who did not hold such a magistracy. The members of the centuriate assembly (the assembly of men under arms that met in the Field of Mars) elected the consuls and praetors. Besides their duties in the city, these magistrates were to lead legions.

3 These powers were granted on January 2, 43 BC. Augustus' *imperium* was that of a praetor and he had the right to hold a military command. As consuls, Hirtius and Pansa, held superior powers.

4 Octavian, Marc Antony, and Marcus Aemilius Lepidus were given supreme powers for five years (November 27, 43–December 31, 38 BC).

5 The inhabitants of a *municipium* were governed by their own laws but had Roman citizenship. In contrast, a *colonia* (colony) was a settlement of Roman citizens.

6 A chair inlaid with ivory (*sella curulis*) was used by consuls, praetors, curule aediles. Hence, the adjective curule implies high distinction. A curule triumph was a procession in honor of a victorious general. The Latin word for general is *imperator*, which is formed from the verb: *imperare*, to give orders, to command.

7 A *fascis* was a bundle of (wooden) rods usually with an axe. A magistrate, who held an *imperium*, would have attendants, *lictors*, assigned to him who carried these bundles, *fasces*. A consul

had twelve, a praetor six such attendants symbolizing their authority and power.

8 Augustus had the powers of a tribune of the people without holding the office. A tribune was sacrosanct and anyone harming him personally or interfering in the performance of a tribune's duties committed a religious crime. Tribunes could veto bills passed in popular assemblies as well as senatorial decrees and acts of magistrates. Most importantly, they could propose laws in the popular assembly. Augustus had received tribunician powers in the settlement of 23 BC when he resigned his consulship.

9 The title is *princeps*. The *princeps senatus* was originally the oldest and preeminent member of the senate whose name appeared first on, i.e. at the head of, the senatorial roster. Hence the word, *prin-ceps = primum caput* (the first head).

10 The *pontifex maximus* was the head of the college of *pontifices* (priests) and as such supervised Rome's public religion. An *augur* was a priest who specialized in the observation and interpretation of bird flight and behavior. The *quindecimviri* (college of fifteen men) were charged with the interpretation of Sibylline sayings and the upkeep of the Sibylline Books as well as the regulation of foreign cults. The *Fratres Arvales* (Arval Brethren) were a college of twelve priests, who made yearly offerings to Dea Dia to ensure a good harvest. The *fetiales* were the priestly college declaring war and peace on behalf of the Roman people. Nothing is known of the *sodales Titii*.

11 A *lustrum* was a purification ritual, which took place after a census was held. It symbolized the newly constituted citizenry.

12 The college of *pontifices*, the augurs, the college of fifteen men, and the college of seven men.

13 A *pulvinar* (plural: *pulvinaria*) was a sacred couch on which images of gods were placed. The gods thus represented were physically present at a religious ceremony and banquet.

14 The Salii were a group of twelve priests. They sang and performed a ritual dance in honor of Mars.

15 This colleague was Lepidus.

16   This gate was at the beginning of the *via Appia* (the Appian Way) at the southern end of the city. When Augustus returned from his campaign of 22–19 BC that brought him to Sicily, Greece, Asia, and Syria, he entered the city through the Capena Gate.

17   The Vestal Virgins were under the auspices of the *pontifex maximus*. The Vestals tended the fire that symbolized the Roman state.

18   Campania is located south of Rome and encompasses the region of the Bay of Naples.

19   The term, *principes iuventutis*, suggests that they are to become *principes* of the whole state.

20   The plebs of the city Rome is meant here.

21   A sesterce was a bronze coin. A soldier serving in the Roman army at the time of Augustus earned 900 sesterces per year. A denarius was worth four sesterces. The monetary reserves captured from Cleopatra formed the source of Augustus' largess in 29 BC. The allocation of 11 BC came on the heel of Augustus' installment as *pontifex maximus*. The generosity of 5 and 2 BC, years in which Augustus also held the consulship, coincide with the introduction of the *princeps'* (adopted) sons to public life.

22   The *curia*, the Chalcidicum, the temple of Apollo and the one to the deified Julius were dedicated in 29/8 BC. The Lupercal was the location where the she-wolf was thought to have found the twins, Romulus and Remus. The *porticus Octavia* was rebuilt in 33 BC. The temple of Jupiter Feretrius was restored in 32 BC, the temple of Jupiter Tonans was dedicated in 22 BC. Quirinus was identified as the deified Romulus. The goddess Minerva formed, with Jupiter and Juno, the Capitoline triad. The penates were household gods. Aeneas, who fled burning Troy, brought the penates of Troy to Italy. Many generations later, his descendants, Romulus and Remus, founded Rome. The Mater Magna (Great Mother) was brought from the Trojan region to Rome in 204 BC. Her temple stood on the Palatine in rather close proximity to Augustus' house.

23   Both bridges are part of the *via Flaminia* (Flaminian Way). The Mulvian bridge crosses the Tiber river north of Rome.

24   We know of seven dates: 29, 28, 16, 12, 7, 2 BC and 6 AD.

25 These were chariot races, gladiatorial games, and theatrical shows.

26 These games were introduced in connection with the inauguration of the temple of Mars Ultor.

27 This naval exhibition occurred in the same year as the inauguration of the temple of Mars Ultor.

28 Augustus alludes to Marc Antony and his (Augustus') victory at Actium in 31 BC.

29 Here Augustus refers obliquely to Sextus Pompeius.

30 The Tyrrhenian Sea.

31 Meroë located on the eastern shore of the Nile in what is now the Sudan; the territory of the Sabaeans as well as Mariba situated in today's Yemen.

32 Cleopatra VII and the three children she had with Marc Antony are meant here. When reorganizing the eastern part of the Roman empire, Marc Antony had allotted Coele-Syria, Cyprus, and part of Cilicia to Cleopatra.

33 After defeating Sextus Pompeius, to whom many slaves had fled and then fought on his side, Octavian took control of Cyrene, Sicily, and Sardinia (38–36 BC).

34 Gabinius lost to the Dalmatians in 48 BC and Vatinius in 44 BC. We do not know about the standards lost in Gaul and Spain. Crassus lost three legions and their standards in Carrhae (Turkey) in 53 BC and there were two additional losses of standards in 40 and 36 BC, in Asia Minor and Armenia respectively. The Parthians returned these standards in 20 BC. The cuirass of the Augustus Primaporta statue depicts this diplomatic victory.

35 The conquest of Pannonia took place from 12 to 9 BC. Likewise, Tiberius crushed a revolt from 6 to 9 AD.

36 When this campaign took place is unclear, sometime between 9 BC and 6 AD.

37 The river Don.

38 The plural form is only in the Greek text.

39 This name ending in -rus cannot be reconstructed.

40 The process of the transfer of power came to a conclusion on January 16, 27 BC. The name Augustus is linguistically related to the verb *augēre*, to increase (in power or might), to enhance,

to promote; the adjective, *augustus-a-um*, translates to: sacred, revered, venerable.

41 The laurel wreath was given to a victor (*imperator*) in battle and the civic crown was given to a person who had saved the life of a citizen.

42 Augustus did not write this addition. Who wrote it, we do not know.

43 The calculation is not exact.

44 The monetary qualifications for senatorial and equestrian rank, the two highest orders, were one million and 400,000 sesterces respectively.

Select Bibliography

Res Gestae Divi Augusti (The Accomplishments of the Deified Augustus)

P. A. Brunt and J. M. Moore, *Res gestae divi Augusti* (Oxford, 1967).

C. Damon, *Res gestae divi Augusti* (Bryn Mawr, Pennsylvania, 1995).

E. S. Ramage, *The nature and purpose of Augustus' res gestae, Historia Einzelschriften*, vol. 54 (Stuttgart, 1987).

R. T. Ridley, "*Res gestae divi Augusti*: the problem of chronology," *Studi S. Calderone*, vol. 2 (Messina, 1986): 265–291.

D. M. Robinson, "The *Res gestae divi Augusti* as recorded on the *monumentum Antiochenum*," *American Journal of Philology* 47 (1926): 1–54.

R. S. Rogers, K. Scott, and M. M. Ward, *Res gestae divi Augusti* (Detroit, [2]1990).

H. Volkmann, *Res gestae divi Augusti. Das Monumentum Ancyranum* (Berlin, [3]1969).

R. Wallace, *Res gestae divi Augusti. Text with notes* (Wauconda, Illinois, 2000).

Politics

A. Alföldi, *Der Vater des Vaterlandes im römischen Denken* (Darmstadt, 1971).

G. Alföldy, *Studi sull' epigrafia augustea e tiberiana di Roma* (Rome, 1992).

T. D. Barnes, "The victories of Augustus," *Journal of Roman Studies* 64 (1974): 21–26.

J. Béranger, "L'accession d'Auguste et l'idéologie du *privatus*," *Palaeologia* 7 (1958): 1–11.

——*Principatus. Études de notions et d'histoire politiques dans l'antiquité greco-romaine* (Geneva, 1973).

J. Bleicken, *Augustus. Eine Biographie* (Berlin, 1998).

B. Bosworth, "Augustus, the *res gestae* and hellenisitic theories of apotheosis. " *Journal of Roman Studies* 89 (1999): 1–18.

G. W. Bowersock, *Augustus and the Greek world* (Oxford, 1965).

A. K. Bowman, E. Champlin, and A. Linott eds., *The Cambridge ancient history*, vol. 10: *The Augustan empire, 43 BC–AD 69* (Cambridge, ²1982).

P. A. Brunt, "The role of the Senate in the Augustan regime," *Classical Quarterly* 34 (1984): 423–444.

——*Roman imperial themes* (Oxford and New York, 1990).

J. M. Carter, *The battle of Actium. The rise and triumph of Augustus Caesar* (London, 1970).

M. P. Charlesworth, "The refusal of divine honours, an Augustan formula," *Papers of the British School at Rome* 15 (1939): 1–10.

K. Christ, "Zur augusteischen Germanienpolitik," *Chiron* 7 (1977): 149–205.

C. J. Classen, "*Virtutes imperatoriae*," *Arctos* 25 (1991): 17–39.

H. M. Cotton and A. Yakobson, "Arcanum imperii," in: G. Clark and T. Rajak, eds., *Philosophy and power in the Graeco-Roman world: Essays in honour of Miriam Griffin* (Oxford, in press).

C. Damon and S. A. Takács, *Senatus consultum de Cn. Pisone patre: text, translation, discussion* (Baltimore, 1999) = *American Journal of Philology* 120. 1.

P. J. Davis, "'Since my part has been well played': conflicting evaluations of Augustus," *Ramus* 28 (1999): 1–15.

D. C. Earl, *The age of Augustus* (London, 1968).

W. Eck, "Augustus' administrative Reformen: Pragmatismus oder systematisches Planen?," *Acta Classica* 29 (1986): 105–120.

——*Die Verwaltung des römischen Reiches in der Hohen Kaiserzeit. Ausgewählte und erweiterte Beiträge* 1 (Basel, 1995).

Select Bibliography

——A. Caballos, and F. Fernández, *Das Senatus Consultum de Cn. Pisone patre* (Munich, 1996).

V. E. Ehrenberg and A. H. M. Jones, *Documents illustrating the reigns of Augustus and Tiberius* (Oxford, reprt. ²1976).

H. Flower, "The tradition of the *spolia opima*: M. Claudius Marcellus and Augustus," *Classical Antiquity* 19. 1 (2000): 34–64.

J. Fugman, "*Mare a praedonibus pacavi* (*Res Gestae* 25. 1)," *Historia* 40 (1991): 307–317.

H. Galsterer, "A man, a book, and a method: Sir Ronald Syme's *Roman Revolution* after fifty years," in K. A. Raaflaub and M. Toher eds., *Between republic and empire. Interpretations of Augustus and his principate* (Berkeley, Los Angeles, and London, 1990): 1–20.

A. Giovannini, "Les pouvoirs d'Auguste de 27 à 23 av. J.-C. Une relecture de l'ordonnance de Kymè de l'an 27 (IK 5, Nr. 17)," *Zeitschrift für Papyrologie und Epigraphik* 124 (1999): 95–106.

K. M. Girardet, "*Imperium 'maius'*. Politische und verfassungsrechtliche Aspekte. Versuch einer Klärung," in A. Giovannini, *La révolution romaine après Ronald Syme. Bilans et perspectives* (Vandoeuvres – Geneva, 2000): 167–227.

R. A. Gurval, *Actium and Augustus: The politics and emotions of civil war* (Ann Arbor, 1995).

C. Habicht, "Die augusteische Zeit und das erste Jahrhundert nach Christi Geburt," in W. den Boer, ed., *Le culte des souverains dans l'empire romain* (Vandoeuvres – Geneva, 1973): 39–99.

J. P. Hallett, "*Perusinae glandes* and the changing image of Augustus," *American Journal of Ancient History* 2 (1977): 151–171.

S. J. Harrison, "Augustus, the poets, and the *spolia opima* (temple of Jupiter Feretrius in Rome)," *Classical Quarterly* 39 (1989): 408–414.

W.-D. Heilmeyer, E. La Rocca, E. Künzel eds., *Kaiser Augustus und die verlorene Republik* (Mainz, 1988).

P. Herrmann, *Der römische Kaisereid. Untersuchungen zu seiner Herkunft und Entwicklung* (Göttingen, 1968).

F. Hurlet, *Les collègues du Prince sous Auguste et Tibère* (Rome, 1997).

A. H. M. Jones, "The *imperium* of Augustus," *Journal of Roman Studies* 41 (1951): 112–119.

——*Augustus* (New York, rprt. 1977).

R. A. Kearsley, "Octavian in the year 32 BC," *Rheinisches Museum* 142 (1999): 52–67.

155

D. Kienast, *Augustus. Princeps und Monarch* (Darmstadt, ³1999).

—— "Augustus und Caesar," *Chiron* 31 (2001): 1–26.

W. K. Lacey, *Augustus and the principate: the evolution of the system* (Leeds, 1996).

—— "Augustus and the principate; the evolution of the system," *Mnemosyne* 52 (1999): 623–634.

B. Levick, "The fall of Julia the Younger," *Latomus* 35 (1976): 301–339.

J. Linderski, "Rome, Aphrodisias and the *res gestae*: the *genera militiae* and the status of Octavian," *Journal of Roman Studies* 74 (1984): 74–80.

—— "Mommsen and Syme: Law and power in the principate of Augustus, in K. A. Raaflaub and M. Toher, eds., *Between republic and empire. Interpretations of Augustus and his principate*, (Berkeley, Los Angeles, and London, 1990): 42–53.

V. Losemann, *Arminius, Varus und die Schlacht im Teutoburger Wald* (Munich, 1998).

R. MacMullen, *Romanization in the time of Augustus* (New Haven, 2000).

F. Millar, "Triumvirate and principate," *Journal of Roman Studies* 63 (1973): 50–67.

—— "Ovid and the *domus Augusta*: Rome seen from Tomoi," *Journal of Roman Studies* 83 (1993): 1–17.

—— and E. Segal, *Caesar Augustus. Seven aspects* (Oxford and New York, 1984).

W. M. Murray and P. M. Petsas, "The spoils of Actium," *Archaeology* 41 (1988): 28–35.

K. A. Raaflaub and M. Toher eds., *Between republic and empire. Interpretations of Augustus and his principate* (Berkeley, Los Angeles, and London, 1990).

—— and L. J. Samons II, "Opposition to Augustus," in: K. A. Raaflaub and M. Toher eds., *Between republic and empire. Interpretations of Augustus and his principate* (Berkeley, Los Angeles, and London, 1990): 417–454.

E. S. Ramage, "Augustus' treatment of Julius Caesar," *Historia* 34 (1985): 223–245.

J. W. Rich and J. H. C. Williams, "*Leges et iura p.r. restituit*": a new aureus of Octavian and his settlement of 28–27 BC," *Numismatic Chronicle* 159 (1999): 169–213.

J.-M. Roddaz, *Marcus Agrippa* (Rome, 1984).

G. C. R. Schmalz, "Athens, Augustus, and the settlement of 21 B.C.," *Greek, Roman and Byzantine Studies* 37 (1996): 381–398.

D. Shotter, "*Principatus ac libertas,*" *Ancient Society* 9 (1978): 235–255.

—— *Augustus Caesar* (London and New York, 1991).

P. Southern, *Augustus* (London and New York, 1998).

R. Syme, *The Roman revolution* (Oxford, 1939).

—— "Imperator Caesar: a study in nomenclature," *Historia* 7 (1958): 172–188. = *Roman Papers* vol. 1 (Oxford and New York, 1979): 361–377.

—— *History in Ovid* (Oxford, 1978).

—— *The Augustan aristocracy* (Oxford, 1986).

W. Turpin, "*Res Gestae* 34.1 and the settlement of 27 B.C.," *Classical Quarterly* 44 (1994): 427–437.

F. Vittinghoff, "*Römische Kolonisation und Bügerrechtspolitik unter Caesar und Augustus,*" Abhandlungen der Akademie Mainz, Geistes- und sozialwissenschaftliche Klasse 1951 No. 14 (Wiesbaden, 1952).

C. M. Wells, *The German policy of Augustus: an examination of the archaeological evidence* (Oxford, 1972).

R. Wiegels and W. Woesler, *Arminius und die Varusschlacht. Geschichte – Mythos – Literatur,* (Paderborn, 1995).

C. Wirszubski, *Libertas as a political idea at Rome during the late republic and early empire* (Cambridge, 1960).

T. P. Wiseman, *New men in the Roman senate 139 B.C.–14 A.D.* (London, 1971).

—— "There went out a decree from Caesar Augustus . . ." *New Testament Studies* 33 (1987): 479–480.

Z. Yavetz, *Plebs and princeps* (Oxford, 1969).

Literature

E. J. Kenney ed. , *The Cambridge history of classical literature*, vol. 2 (Cambridge and New York, 1982).

A. Powel ed., *Roman poetry and propaganda in the age of Augustus* (London, 1992).

M. Santirocco, "Horace and Augustan ideology," *Arethusa* 28 (1995): 225–243.

P. White, *Promised verse. Poets in the society of Augustan Rome* (Cambridge, 1993).

T. Woodman and D. West eds., *Poetry and politics in the age of Augustus* (Cambridge, 1984).

Architecture / Art / Numismatics

E. Buchner, "*Solarium Augusti* und *Ara Pacis*," *Römische Mitteilungen* 83 (1976): 319–365.

——"Ein Kanal für Obelisken: Neues vom Mausoleum des Augustus in Rom," *Antike Welt* 27 (1996): 161–168.

D. Favro, *The urban image of Augustan Rome* (New York, 1996).

M. D. Fullerton, "The *domus Augusti* in imperial iconography of 13–12 B.C.," *American Journal of Archaeology* 89 (1985): 473–483.

K. Galinsky, *Augustan culture. An interpretive introduction* (Princeton, 1996).

P. Gros, *Aurea templa. Recherches sur l'architecture religieuse de Rome à l'époque d'Auguste*, (Rome, 1976).

N. Hannestadt, *Roman art and imperial policy* (Aarhus, 1986).

A. L. Kuttner, *Dynasty and empire in the age of Augustus: the case of the Boscoreale Cups* (Berkeley, 1995).

J. C. Reeder, "The statue of Augustus from Prima Porta, the underground complex, and the omen of the *gallina alba*," *American Journal of Philology* 118 (1997): 89–118.

J. W. Rich, "Augustus's Parthian honours, the temple of Mars Ultor and the arch in the *forum Romanum*," *Papers of the British School at Rome* 66 (1998): 71–128.

C. H. V. Sutherland, *Coinage in Roman imperial policy 31 B.C. – A.D. 68* (London, 1951).

——*The Roman imperial coinage*, vol. 1 (London, 1984).

A. Wallace-Hadrill, "Image and authority in the coinage of Augustus." *Journal of Roman Studies* 76 (1986): 66–87.

——*Augustan Rome* (London, 1993).

P. Zanker, *The power of images in the age of Augustus*, trans. A. Shapiro (Ann Arbor, 1988).

Index

Index